D1329231

# DISCOVERY WALKS:
# Birmingham & the
# Black Country

## Brian Conduit

**Published by** Sigma Leisure – an imprint of
Sigma Press, 1 South Oak Lane, Wilmslow, Cheshire SK9 6AR, England.

**British Library Cataloguing in Publication Data**
A CIP record for this book is available from the British Library.

**ISBN:** 1-85058-747-7

**Typesetting and Design by:** Sigma Press, Wilmslow, Cheshire.

**Cover photographs:** clockwise from top left: Lichfield Cathedral; Cobb's Engine House, Bumble Hole; Brindleyplace, Birmingham city centre

**Maps:** Jeremy Semmens

**Printed by:** MFP Design and Print

**Disclaimer:** the information in this book is given in good faith and is believed to be correct at the time of publication. No responsibility is accepted by either the author or publisher for errors or omissions, or for any loss or injury howsoever caused. Only you can judge your own fitness, competence and experience.

# Preface

When I was a boy growing up in Birmingham in the 1940s and 50s, it would have been considered ludicrous for someone to write a guide-book encouraging people to go walking in Birmingham and the Black Country. But at that time, it would also have been regarded as inconceivable that one day Birmingham, Wolverhampton, Walsall and Dudley would all have tourist information centres and that the Black Country canals would become recreational assets. Times change and, over the past half-century, this area has seen more changes than most.

Probably the biggest change of all is that the Black Country is no longer black. The coal mines have long since closed down and much of the heavy industry for which the region was once famous – and from which it gets its name – has gone. Countless factories and furnaces no longer pour black smoke into the atmosphere and the result is that the area is now much cleaner and greener. The many canals, once little more than filthy and neglected backwaters, have been restored, cleaned up and transformed into major amenities. Ranked among the most outstanding engineering triumphs of the Industrial Revolution, their towpaths make excellent walking routes: flat, easy to follow, quiet – even in the midst of large towns and busy main roads – and with plenty of historic and architectural appeal. Near the canals, many former derelict industrial sites are now country parks or nature reserves.

Birmingham has become a major international conference centre and in recent years its city centre – much of it pedestrianised – has been vastly improved and made much more attractive and appealing. Imposing new buildings and spacious squares accompany the fine civic monuments to the city's illustrious Victorian past. Some of its heritage was destroyed in the ruthless purge of the 1960s but now there is a greater emphasis on conservation. The historic Jewellery Quarter, the elegant Victorian suburb of Edgbaston and the model industrial village of Bournville are all worth exploring, as well as the city's well-publicised and extensive canal network. Added to this, Birmingham has a large number of fine parks, several country parks and invaluable 'green fingers' along the banks of some of its small rivers and streams.

This walking guide is not just confined to Birmingham and the Black Country. It includes town walks in two other cities and routes in the surrounding rural areas. Coventry is one of the cities. Largely rebuilt after extensive wartime destruction and famed for its striking modern cathedral, it retains some of its earlier buildings. The other city is Lichfield, dominated by its medieval, three-spired cathedral. Some of the rural walks take you to places that have long been traditional weekend and bank holiday destinations for the people of Birmingham and the Black Country. Among these are the Clent and Lickey hills, Kinver Edge, Cannock Chase and Sutton Park. Even within the heavily industrialised and urbanised zone, there were always substantial oases of greenery and the decline of heavy industry and subsequent reclamation of former areas of dereliction is adding to these. Both local people and visitors to the region may well be surprised by what this part of England has to offer. It makes a change from some of the more obvious tourist areas and its unique blend of urban, rural and semi-rural landscapes and rich heritage – especially its industrial past – is well worth exploring. The best way to do this is by foot.

*Brian Conduit*

## Acknowledgements

I have acquired much valuable advice and many useful leaflets from the various tourist information centres throughout the region and I am grateful for the help received from the Birmingham Park Rangers in Cannon Hill Park, regarding the Rea Valley Cycle Route, and from the Project Kingfisher Ranger Service.

# Contents

## The Walks

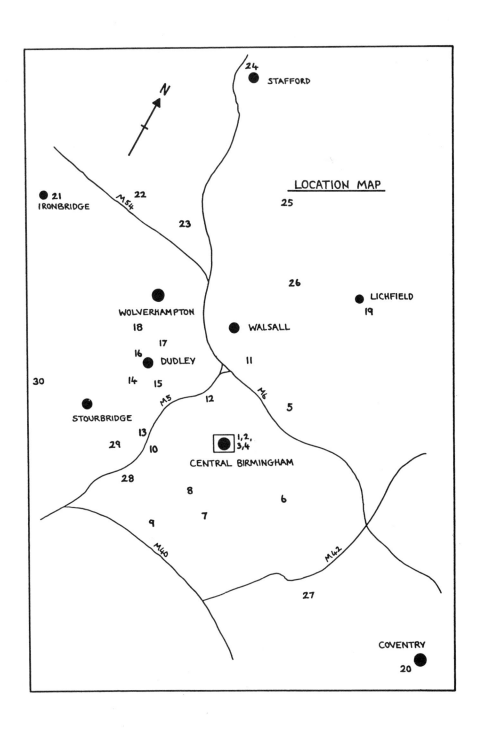

LOCATION MAP

N

24 STAFFORD

21 IRONBRIDGE

M54 22

23

25

26

LICHFIELD 19

WOLVERHAMPTON 18

WALSALL

17

16 DUDLEY

11

30

14 15

M5

12

M6

5

STOURBRIDGE

13

29

10

1,2, 3,4

CENTRAL BIRMINGHAM

28

8

6

9

7

M40

M42

27

COVENTRY 20

# Introduction

In 1868 Elihu Burritt, the American consul in Birmingham at the time, published a book called 'Walks in the Black Country and Its Green Border-Land'. The book arose out of his consular duties, which required that he travelled extensively throughout the West Midlands and submitted regular reports to the Department of State in Washington. But this book was far more detailed than the normal consular report and was the outcome of his deep interest in and love for the area. He was fascinated by both Birmingham, which was then growing rapidly, and the Black Country, then at the height of its industrial greatness, but he also greatly admired their rural setting. He wrote: 'The Black Country is beautifully framed by a Green Border-Land, and that border is rich and redolent with two beautiful wealths – the sweet life of Nature's happiest springs and summers, and the hive and romance of England's happiest industries'. However much this is a typical piece of Victorian over-exaggeration, it does convey something of the varied appeal and the differing aspects of the landscape of the region. Like Elihu Burritt's book, this walking guide is not just about Birmingham and the Black Country but also explores the 'Green Border-Land' that surrounds the urban and industrial zone. Since he wrote his book, there have been both gains and losses. Birmingham's suburbs have spread out far more to devour much formerly green and unspoilt countryside and Burritt would have found the noise of traffic on the region's motorways intolerable. On the other hand, there is less noise from the hundreds of forges and furnaces that used to cover the Black Country, the black smoke – which gave the region its nickname – no longer pours into the atmosphere, the area is indisputably cleaner and greener and Birmingham has become a more impressive and pedestrian-friendly city, with much fine modern architecture to complement its legacy of Victorian buildings.

Every Brummie will tell you that the city has more miles of canals than Venice, which may well be true, and these canals are one of the main reasons for the remarkable growth of what was once an insignificant village into Britain's second city and one of the world's great manufacturing centres. In the Domesday Book, Birmingham was worth less than many of its close neighbours who have now become its suburbs. By Tudor times it had acquired a reputation for making swords and metal goods, using local coal and iron from the Black Country, and in the Civil War between Charles I and Parliament it manufactured arms for the Parliamentary armies. The rise of Birmingham and the Black Country into a major manufacturing area came during the 18th century with the onset of the Industrial Revolution. There were two major turning points. One was the smelting of iron ore with coke instead of charcoal, first achieved by Abraham Darby at his Coalbrookdale works in Shropshire in 1709. By using coal and thus freeing the iron industry from its dependence on timber, iron and its associated metal industries could expand and utilise the resources of the South Staffordshire coalfield – i.e. the Black Country. The second turning point was the partnership between Matthew Boulton and James Watt, which produced the first successful steam engine at Boulton's Soho Manufactory in Birmingham in the 1780s. For the next quarter of a century or so, Boulton and Watt supplied the rest of the world with steam engines.

The one great disadvantage of the area was that it lacked rivers and land transport was very slow and expensive at the time. It was to overcome this problem that the local industrialists developed the canal network. Beginning with the Main Line Canal between Birmingham and Wolverhampton in 1767, canals were constructed all over the region during the following half century, firstly to link the Black Country with Birmingham and then to link the region with the rest of the country, especially with the ports of London, Bristol, Liverpool and Hull. Birmingham became the hub England's waterway network and much of its trade flowed out from Gas Street Basin in the centre of the city. Burritt described the canals of the Black Country as 'filled with water black as the long sharp boats it floats, crossing each other here and there in the thick of the furnaces'. Now they are mainly used for recreation and many of their towpaths provide green, quiet, attractive and interesting walking routes through the heart of what were once noisy and dirty industrial areas.

The Birmingham and Black Country region was at its manufacturing height in the Victorian period and up to the First World War when it supplied the world with a vast array of metal goods. In the Black Country, many of the towns had their specialised trade – locks at Willenhall, needles at Redditch, leather at Walsall, glass at Stourbridge etc. Elihu Burritt vividly conveys what the region was like at the time in the opening sentence of his book: 'The Black Country, black by day and red by night, cannot be matched for vast and varied production, by any other space of equal radius on the surface of the globe'.

In the late 19th century, under the energetic leadership of Joseph Chamberlain and other local dignitaries, Birmingham pioneered a number of civic improvements, including slum clearance, provision of gas and water and educational advancement, which put it in the forefront of municipal enterprise. In 1890 one visitor described it as 'the best governed city in the world'. Around this time it became a city, acquired a new university and became the seat of a diocese. As the city expanded, it engulfed a number of small villages into its suburbs. Many of these have managed to retain something of their village atmosphere, including medieval churches and some old inns. Also Birmingham's suburbs are well endowed with parks and other open spaces which create opportunities for pleasant walks.

Beyond the industrial zone, Burritt wrote about a 'green velvet binding' and within that 'binding' are many places that became popular destinations for the people of the crowded city and adjoining smoky industrial towns. On summer weekends and bank holidays, thousands flocked to the Lickey and Clent hills, Kinver Edge, Sutton Park and Cannock Chase by bus, tram, train, bike or on foot. Nowadays people come mainly by car but both locals and visitors to the area are lucky to have such fine walking areas near at hand.

The coal and iron mines have long since closed, much of the heavy industry has gone and the region is trying to forge a new future. Birmingham is transforming itself into a major international conference and cultural centre and the Black Country is trying to attract new hi-tech industries. In this new, largely post-industrial era, tourism – including attracting walkers into the area – will play an increasingly important role.

The 30 walks in this guide introduce you both to the heritage and fine scenery of the area and try to illustrate some of the changes. They are as varied a collection as is possible to imagine, comprising a mixture of urban, suburban, semi-rural and rural routes. There could be no greater contrast than the city walks along the canal from the centre of Birmingham to Aston and Smethwick, and the country walks around Berkswell and Brewood. To add to the variety, two historic town walks in Lichfield and Coventry are included. Although at first glance an unlikely walking venue, there is much to explore and discover in and around Britain's second city and one of the best places in which to make a start and get a flavour of the area is the Black Country Museum near Dudley. Here its rich and varied heritage is preserved and portrayed for all to enjoy and experience.

# General Information

The walks include many sites of historic interest – including museums, castles, churches and great houses. You will no doubt wish to visit some of these, it is disappointing if you find them closed. Therefore, it is important to check opening times – which vary considerably. The nearest tourist information centres will provide you with details, as well as up-to-date information on public transport and hotel, guest house and bed and breakfast accommodation.

## Local Tourist Information Centres

| | |
|---|---|
| Birmingham | 0121 643 2514 |
| | 0121 780 4321 |
| | 0121 693 6300 |
| Coventry | 01203 832303/832304 |
| Dudley | 01384 812830 |
| Ironbridge | 01952 432166 |
| Lichfield | 01543 252109 |
| Merry Hill | 01384 487911 |
| Solihull | 0121 704 6130/6134 |
| Stafford | 01785 240204 |
| Walsall | 01922 653110 |
| Wolverhampton | 01902 312051 |

For information on public transport in West Midlands county, phone Centro Hotline 0121 200 2700 (for Coventry 01203 559 559)

## Useful Addresses

**Heart of England Tourist Board**, Woodside, Larkhill Road, Worcester WR5 2EF. Tel: 01905 763436

**English Heritage**, Customer Services, PO Box 9019, London W1A 0JA. Tel: 0171 9733434

**Countryside Commission**, John Dower House, Crescent Place, Cheltenham, Gloucestershire GL50 3RA. Tel: 01242 521381

**Ramblers' Association**, 2nd Floor, Camelford House, 87-90 Albert Embankment, London SE1 7TW. Tel: 020 7339 8500

**Birmingham and Black Country Canals**, Bradley Lane, Bilston, West Midlands WV14 8DW. Tel: 01902 409010
**Black Country Museum**, Tipton Road, Dudley, West Midlands DY1 4SQ. Tel: 0121 557 9643

## The Country Code

Please observe this when walking in the countryside:

* Enjoy the countryside and respect its life and work

* Guard against all risk of fire

* Take your litter home

* Fasten all gates

* Help to keep all water clean

* Keep your dogs under control

* Protect wildlife, plants and trees

* Keep to public paths across farmland

* Take special care on country roads

* Leave livestock, crops and machinery alone

* Make no unnecessary noise

* Use gates and stiles to cross fences, hedges and walls

# 1. City Centre and Jewellery Quarter

**Start:** Victoria Square – grid ref. 067868

**Distance:** 3½ miles (5.6km)

**Category:** Easy

**Parking:** Birmingham

**Refreshments:** Plenty of pubs, cafés and restaurants in Birmingham city centre and the Jewellery Quarter

**Terrain:** Easy town walking

**Maps:** Pick up a street map from the Visitor Information Centres in Victoria Square or City Arcade

**Public transport:** Central Birmingham is served by buses and trains from all the surrounding towns and has coach and rail links with all parts of the country

## Discover:

A substantial slice of Birmingham's history is encountered on this walk and there is a varied mixture of both old and new. It takes in some of the city's imposing Victorian civic monuments, the exciting new developments around Centenary Square and the International Convention Centre, an attractive stretch of refurbished canal and a fascinating walk through part of the historic Jewellery Quarter. The walk also includes Birmingham Cathedral and the city's only remaining Georgian square.

## Route Directions:

Start by facing the Council House and pass between it and the Town Hall into Chamberlain Square (A). Bear left to the Chamberlain Fountain, ascend the steps beyond and enter Paradise Forum. Walk through it, continue along Centenary Way and across Centenary Square into the International Convention Centre (B) and pass through it to reach the canal opposite a footbridge.

If the International Convention Centre is closed, walk along Broad Street to the left of it, descend steps to the canal and turn right to the footbridge.

Cross the footbridge and keep ahead to explore the Brindleyplace development (C). Return to the footbridge, descend steps to the left of it

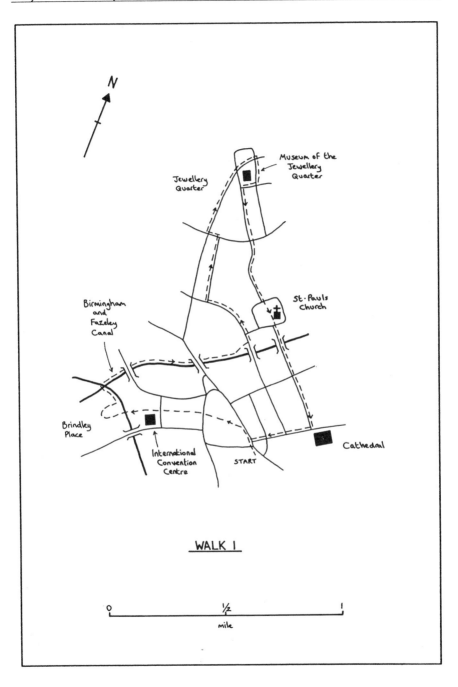

N

Museum of the
Jewellery
Quarter

Jewellery
Quarter

St·Pauls
Church

Birmingham
and
Fazeley
Canal

Brindley
Place

International
Convention
Centre

START

Cathedral

WALK 1

0                    ½                    1
                   mile

and turn left beside the canal, passing the National Sea Life Centre. Turn right to cross a footbridge at Deep Cutting Junction to the National Indoor Arena, turn sharp left down steps in front of it and at the bottom turn left to continue beside the Birmingham and Fazeley Canal (D).

Descend by the Farmers Bridge Locks and keep by the canal as far as Newhall Street Bridge. Just before going under the bridge, turn left up steps – there is a sign to the Jewellery Quarter here – and turn left along Newhall Street. Over to the right is the Birmingham Assay Office (E). Follow the road to the left to continue along Graham Street into the Jewellery Quarter. Turn right into Vittoria Street but a few yards detour ahead brings you to the Argent Centre on the corner of Frederick Street, a particularly fine example of 'Jewellery Quarter architecture' (F). Vittoria Street has some good Victorian workshops and at the T-junction at the end of it – in front of the Hockley Centre (Big Peg) – turn left to the Chamberlain Clock Tower, built in 1903 to commemorate Joseph Chamberlain's visit to South Africa. He was Colonial Secretary at the time, as well as MP for this area of Birmingham.

Turn right along Vyse Street, passing Warstone Lane cemetery on the left, to the Museum of the Jewellery Quarter (G). Just beyond the museum, turn right along Branston Street, right again into Hockley Street and at the road junction by the Jeweller's Arms and the Jewellery Business Centre, turn left into Spencer Street. Bear right at a junction to continue along Caroline Street into St Paul's Square (H). Keep ahead across the churchyard and along Ludgate Hill, cross the footbridge over Great Charles Street and continue up Church Street to emerge into Colmore Row opposite the cathedral (J). Turn right to return to Victoria Square.

## Features of Interest:

**A.** Many of the surviving civic monuments of the Victorian era, when Birmingham was the greatest manufacturing city in the world, are grouped round Victoria Square and the adjoining Chamberlain Square. Finest of these are the Town Hall, an imitation Roman temple completed in 1834, and the Council House, built in a Renaissance style in the 1870s. Victoria Square was imaginatively landscaped in the 1990s, making the most of its sloping position, with an impressive cascading fountain, locally nicknamed 'the floosie in the jacuzzi', and new sculptures. Around the corner in Chamberlain Square is the City Museum and Art Gallery, opened in 1885. The

Chamberlain Fountain in the middle of the square was erected in honour of Joseph Chamberlain, three times mayor in the 1870s, who did so much to improve the Victorian city by instigating slum clearance schemes, bringing in fresh water supplies and promoting the foundation of the university.

**B.** The spacious Centenary Square was laid out in 1989 to commemorate Birmingham's centenary as a borough and around it are buildings from various periods. Baskerville House and the Hall of Memory – the city's war memorial – were both built in the inter-war years. The Repertory Theatre was erected in the 1960s and the International Convention Centre was opened in 1991. The latter incorporates Symphony Hall, one of the world's finest concert halls.

**C.** Brindleyplace is an ambitious new development – now nearing completion – that embraces a range of modern buildings of varied architectural styles that all seem to harmonise. These buildings include restaurants, pubs, wine bars, office buildings and the National Sea Life Centre. In addition a Victorian school has been transformed into the Ikon Gallery, a venue for new art. The scene is enhanced by fountains and sculptures and the whole area has a pleasantly relaxed and almost continental atmosphere.

**D.** The Birmingham and Fazeley Canal, constructed by Smeaton and completed in 1789, was built to link Birmingham with the canals and rivers to the north and east, thus opening up new waterway routes.

**E.** The Birmingham Assay Office, reputedly the largest in the world, has been in existence since 1773.

**F.** The Jewellery Quarter is one of the most distinctive manufacturing areas of any of Britain's major provincial cities and it has been the centre of the jewellery trade for over 200 years. The precious metals industry grew out of the toy trades – the manufacture of trinkets and small boxes – for which Birmingham was well known. As the industry expanded and became more and more concentrated within this relatively small area, the population grew and the gardens of the houses became built over with numerous workshops. The Quarter was at its height in the Victorian era and on the eve of the First World War, over 30,000 people were employed here. Since the 1980s, it has become a retail as well as a manufacturing area.

**G.** The Museum of the Jewellery Quarter is based on the workshops and offices of Smith and Pepper, former jewellery manufacturers. It is a living museum which not only displays the history of the industry in this area but also enables you to see skilled jewellers at work.

**H.** Dignified brick buildings line St Paul's Square, Birmingham's only remaining Georgian square. In the middle of it is St Paul's church, built in the 1770s and formerly known as the 'Jewellers Church' because of its close links with the industry.

**J.** Birmingham Cathedral, built as a parish church in the early 18th century by Thomas Archer, is a fine example of the Baroque style. It was chosen as the cathedral of the new diocese of Birmingham in 1905. The interior is noted for the four superb stained glass windows by Burne-Jones, a native of the city.

Birmingham's 18th-century cathedral

# 2. Aston Junction, Aston Hall and Digbeth

**Start:** Victoria Square – grid ref. 067868

**Distance:** The full walk is 6½ miles (10.5km); the shorter version, which omits the extension to Aston Hall, is 3½ miles (5.6km)

**Category:** Easy

**Parking:** Birmingham

**Refreshments:** Plenty of pubs, cafés and restaurants in Birmingham city centre, Potters Restaurant and Bar beside canal near Aston Junction, Waterfront Bar and Restaurant at Aston Cross (by Rocky Lane Bridge), pubs and cafés at Digbeth

**Terrain:** Mostly along canal towpaths, with some road walking

**OS Maps:** Landranger 139, Explorer 220

**Public transport:** Central Birmingham is served by buses and trains from all the surrounding towns and has coach and rail links with all parts of the country

## Discover:

This is a wholly urban and canal-based walk which reveals a fascinating mixture of old and new. It starts by taking you along the Birmingham and Fazeley Canal to Aston Junction. From there you keep by the canal and along roads to the 17<sup>th</sup>-century Aston Hall, Birmingham's finest historic building. After returning to Aston Junction, you continue beside the Digbeth Branch Canal into Digbeth and then through the Bull Ring to return to the start.

## Route Directions:

Facing the Council House, turn right along Colmore Row and turn left down Newhall Street to the bridge over the Birmingham and Fazeley Canal. After crossing the bridge, turn left down steps and left again onto the towpath (A). The towpath descends beside part of the Farmers Bridge Flight of Locks and passes under tunnels and between buildings to reach Aston Junction (B) – just after passing Aston Road Bridge.

For the short walk, bear left off the towpath here and turn right over a cast iron bridge to continue by the Digbeth Branch Canal. For the full walk to Aston Hall, continue along the towpath of the Birmingham and Fazeley Canal. You pass under the cast iron bridge and then cross a brick bridge to walk along the opposite bank of the canal, all the time following signs to Salford Junction. Leave the canal by locks and a cottage – this is at the bridge after Rocky Lane Bridge – and turn left over the bridge. At a roundabout, keep ahead along Church Road, cross Lichfield Road and pass under the Aston Expressway to Aston church.

Immediately bear left onto a tarmac path into Aston Park and at a path junction, turn left up to Aston Hall (C).

From here retrace your steps to Aston Junction but instead of crossing the brick bridge to the other side, keep ahead to the cast iron bridge and turn left, in the Love Lane and Camp Hill direction, to continue along the towpath of the Digbeth Branch Canal. To the right is Aston Science Park. Pass under Ashted Tunnel, descend alongside Ashted Locks, pass under a railway tunnel and soon the Rotunda and the spire of St Martin's church in the Bull Ring are seen ahead. After passing under the railway tunnel, you reach a canal junction where you bear left uphill, in the Fazeley Street direction, to cross the Grand Union Canal. Continue beside the Digbeth Basin, leave the canal in front of the next bridge and head up to a road. Turn right along Fazeley Street, in the City Centre direction, turn left into New Canal Street, turn right along Bordesley Street and take the first turning on the left (Allison Street) (D). Pass under a railway viaduct – note the urinal in the arch – and keep ahead to Digbeth. Cross the busy road and turn right into the Bull Ring, passing St Martin's church (E). Following signs to the Central Shopping Area, ascend steps into New Street and turn left to return to Victoria Square. NB. At the time of publication, the Bull Ring is being redeveloped and these route directions may have become redundant. Simply follow current signs to New Street or the Central Shopping Area.

## Features of Interest:

**A.** For details of the Birmingham and Fazeley Canal, see Walk 1.

**B.** Aston Junction is the meeting place of the Birmingham and Fazeley and Digbeth Branch canals. The Digbeth Branch Canal was cut in 1799 and provides a direct link with the Grand Union Canal at Bordesley.

**C.** Looking down the tree-lined avenue in Aston Park from the hall to the tower and spire of the church, and provided you can close your

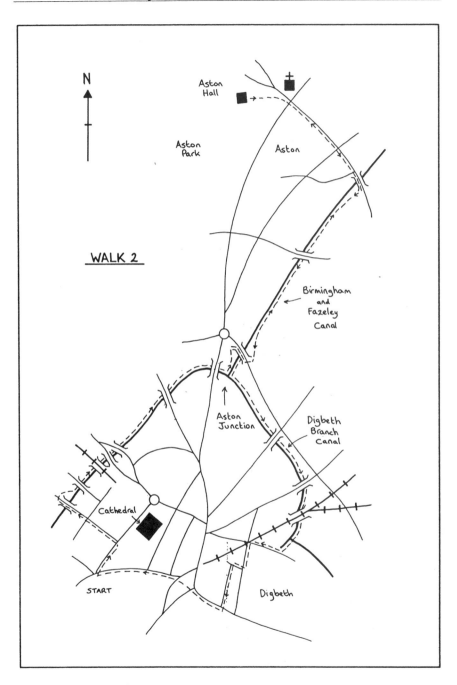

ears to the noise of traffic on the expressway, it is still almost possible to envisage Aston as a rural hamlet around the hall and church which are – in the traditional English manner – in close proximity. As a result of the growth of Birmingham in the 19th and 20th centuries, Aston Hall is now surrounded by housing estates, industry, a busy expressway and Villa Park football ground but the park still gives it a noble setting. It is an outstanding example of a large Jaco-

Aston Hall

bean country house and was built between 1618 and 1635 for Sir Thomas Holte. During the Civil War it was besieged by Parliamentary troops and the scars left by cannon shot can still be seen on the stairs. Pride of place is the impressive Long Gallery and there is a fine collection of furniture, paintings, ornaments and textiles. Aston church is mentioned in Domesday Book but, except for the 15th-century tower and spire, the present church was mainly rebuilt in the 19th century.

**D.** The Digbeth area was at the heart of medieval Birmingham, based around the River Rea. The construction of the canals in the 18th century and the coming of the railways in the 19th century turned it into a busy commercial and industrial area, with warehouses, factories and wharves. Many impressive Victorian buildings remain, as do several cast iron, continental-type urinals, apparently provided as a result of the numerous pubs that used to be around here!

E. St Martin's, the mother church of Birmingham, towers above the Bull Ring and there has been a church on the site since the Middle Ages. Although the present church was almost entirely rebuilt in 1873, it contains tombs of some of the de Bermingham family, the medieval lords of the manor. There have been markets in the Bull Ring since the 12th century and it has always been a bustling and characterful area, much loved by Brummies. It was comprehensively redeveloped in the 1960s – not without considerable controversy – and it is now being rebuilt again. We shall await the results with interest.

# 3. Edgbaston, Birmingham University and Bournville

**Start:** Gas Street Basin – grid ref. 062866

**Finish:** Bournville, junction of Bournville Lane and Bristol Road – grid ref. 035814

**Distance:** 5½ miles (8.9km)

**Category:** Easy

**Parking:** Birmingham

**Refreshments:** Plenty of pubs, cafés and restaurants in Birmingham city centre

**Terrain:** Mostly along a canal towpath, with a final section across parkland

**OS Maps:** Landranger 139, Explorer 220

**Public transport:** Central Birmingham is served by buses and trains from all the surrounding towns and has coach and rail links with all parts of the country

## Discover:

Most of this route follows the towpath of the Worcester and Birmingham Canal from Gas Street Basin in the heart of Birmingham to Bournville. It is surprising how quickly and easily you escape from the city centre into the peaceful and semi-rural surroundings of leafy Edgbaston, the city's most prestigious suburb, and the walk finishes with a stroll through Bournville, the model industrial village created by the Cadbury family. You might well wish to allow time for a visit to Cadbury World before returning to Birmingham city centre.

## Route Directions:

Looking across Gas Street Basin (A) to the James Brindley pub, turn right along the towpath of the Worcester and Birmingham Canal (B). Follow it around a right angle bend and continue along the towpath for nearly 4 miles (6.4km) as far as Bournville station. For most of the way you keep parallel with the railway line on the right and the surroundings quickly become surprisingly rural, considering the proximity of Birmingham city centre. There are good views of the elegant houses and

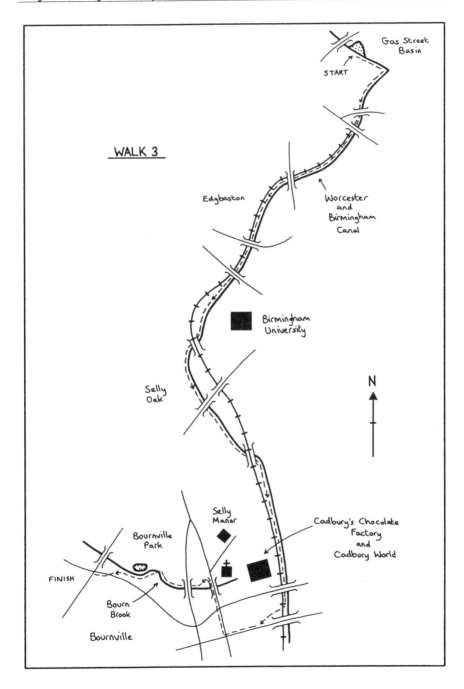

Gas Street
Basin

START

WALK 3

Edgbaston

Worcester
and
Birmingham
Canal

Birmingham
University

N

Selly
Oak

Selly
Manor

Cadbury's Chocolate
Factory
and
Cadbury World

Bournville
Park

FINISH

Bourn
Brook

Bournville

green spaces of Edgbaston (C) and soon after passing under Edgbaston Tunnel – 105 yards (96m) long – you reach a small picnic area from where you look across towards the Botanical Gardens. Later the route passes by some of the University Halls of Residence, then the university itself, dominated by the Chamberlain Tower (D) and continues on through the more industrial surroundings of Selly Oak.

About 1 mile (1.6km) beyond Selly Oak, you see the Cadbury chocolate factory over to the right and at Bournville station you leave the canal by ascending a ramp. Turn right to cross both the canal and the railway line and continue along Mary Vale Road, passing almshouses (1897) on the right, to a crossroads. Turn right and head down into Bournville village centre. After crossing Bourn Brook, the route continues to the left through Bournville Park but keep ahead past the church to Bournville Green. Around this village green is the Carillon and Selly Manor and in the middle is the Carillon Visitor Centre (E). After entering the park, walk along the main tarmac path to emerge onto Oaktree Lane, turn left to cross Bourn Brook, turn right onto another tarmac path to recross it and continue through the park. Cross a road, keep ahead – still by the brook and later by a pool on the right – to emerge onto Bournville Lane. Turn right up to the main Bristol Road where buses will take you back to Birmingham city centre.

## Features of Interest:

**A.** Once the hub of Birmingham's canal network, Gas Street Basin has been revitalised in recent years and is now an attractive and popular marina and waterside area surrounded by pubs, restaurants, wine bars and night clubs. In the 18th century much of Birmingham's trade flowed out from here from the many wharves and warehouses and it was the meeting place of two canal systems. A seven-foot wide barrier, the Worcester Bar, separated the Worcester and Birmingham Canal from the Birmingham Canal Navigations and until the construction of a stop lock in 1815, goods had to be hauled from one to the other.

**B.** Construction of the Worcester and Birmingham Canal began in 1792 and was finally completed in 1815. It linked the industrial Midlands with the River Severn and the Bristol Channel.

**C.** Edgbaston is Birmingham's most prestigious suburb. Cricket lovers will automatically think of the Test Match ground but it is regarded as one of England's finest examples of a residential Victorian suburb with a wealth of imposing Regency and Victorian villas, some of which are seen from the canal towpath. It was the Calthorpe family, lords of the manor, who did much to retain its spacious and leafy character by preventing the usual urban sprawl of the Victorian period.

D. The buildings of Birmingham University are dominated by the Chamberlain Tower (Joe), 325 feet (99m) high and modelled on the campanile at Siena. Founded in 1900, the university was originally based in the city centre but this site at Edgbaston was developed from 1909 onwards.

E. It was in 1879 that Richard and George Cadbury chose this site for the construction of their new chocolate factory. Proximity to the canal was one factor which influenced their choice but fresh air and pleasant surroundings, away from the smoke and grime of Birmingham, was another. The factory was nicknamed 'the factory in the garden' and for many years the canal was used to transport its products. George Cadbury also founded the model village of Bournville for his workers. It was designed to resemble a traditional English village and the workers were provided with decent houses, including

The village green at Bournville

their own gardens, a rarity at the time in working class housing. The structure on the village green, now the Carillon Visitor Centre, was originally a Silver Wedding present from a grateful workforce to George Cadbury and his wife. The traditional aspect of the village is further emphasised by the presence of two medieval, half-timbered buildings at one corner. These are Selly Manor and the smaller Minworth Greaves, both saved from demolition and re-sited here from other parts of the city.

The immensely popular visitor attraction of Cadbury World, a must for all those who like chocolate, tells the story of chocolate manufacture and the history of Bournville and the Cadburys.

# 4. Gas Street Basin to Galton Valley

**Start:** Gas Street Basin – grid ref. 062866

**Finish:** Smethwick, Galton Bridge Station – grid ref. 015894

**Distance:** 4½ miles (7.2km)

**Category:** Easy

**Parking:** Birmingham

**Refreshments:** Plenty of pubs, cafés and restaurants in Birmingham city centre

**Terrain:** Entirely on canal towpaths

**OS Maps:** Landranger 139, Explorer 220

**Public transport:** Central Birmingham is served by buses and trains from all the surrounding towns and has coach and rail links with all parts of the country

---

## Discover:

The walk follows the New Main Line Canal between Birmingham and Wolverhampton, and one of the loops of the parallel Old Main Line, from the heart of Birmingham to Smethwick, a pleasant and perhaps surprisingly green corridor through a heavily urbanised and industrialised part of the city – Ladywood and Winson Green – that borders the Black Country. There is some outstanding canal architecture to appreciate, including some attractive iron bridges, and the route goes through the Galton Valley Canal Heritage Area, finishing at the striking Galton Bridge.

## Route Directions:

Looking across Gas Street Basin (A) to the James Brindley pub, turn left beside the canal, pass under Broad Street Tunnel and continue past Brindleyplace and the National Sea Life Centre – the International Convention Centre is on the opposite side of the canal (B) – to the National Indoor Arena. After crossing a bridge over the Oozells Street Loop, keep along the left bank of the New Main Line Canal for just under 1 mile (1.6km) as far as Rotton Park Junction (C).

At the junction, turn right to cross an iron bridge over the canal, turn right on the other side, cross a bridge over the Old Main Line Canal and turn first sharp right and then right again to pass under the bridge just crossed. Now continue along the right bank of the Old Main Line Canal, following it around a long left curve and crossing the Soho Branch Canal, to Winson Green Junction where you rejoin the New Main Line. Turn right along its right bank to Smethwick Junction, where the canal divides again. Pass under one bridge, turn left over the next one and at a fork, and take the left-hand path to continue along the right bank of the canal. Pass under an aqueduct and at the next bridge (Brasshouse Bridge) – a high brick structure – turn sharp right up steps to the Old Main Line and turn left up to a road between twin canal bridges. Cross over, go down the steps opposite and continue beside the canal to Smethwick Pumping Station (D). Just beyond it, turn left down steps to the New Main Line again and turn right to follow it through the Galton Valley.

After passing under a tunnel you reach the imposing Galton Bridge (E). Turn sharp right up a wooded path which bends sharp left up to a road and turn left to cross the pedestrianised bridge to a main road. Smethwick Galton Bridge Station is just to the right and from here you can catch either a train or the 87 bus back to Birmingham city centre.

## Features of Interest:

**A.** For details of Gas Street Basin see Walk 3

**B.** For details of Brindleyplace and the International Convention Centre see Walk 1

**C.** At Rotton Park Junction the Old Main Line Canal does a loop and rejoins the New Main Line Canal, which continues in a straight line, at Winson Green Junction. The canals part again at Smethwick Junction and for the remainder of the walk run parallel to and scarcely more than a few yards away from each other. For details on the history of the two canals – one built by Brindley and the other by Telford – see Walk 17

**D.** Smethwick New Pumping Station is in the heart of the Galton Valley Canal Heritage Area and is a branch of the Canal Centre – the main building is just along Brasshouse Lane. It is situated between the two canals and was used to raise water from one level to the other. The Old Main Line Canal is at a higher level because at Smethwick Junction it climbs via locks. In contrast, Telford's New Main Line Canal

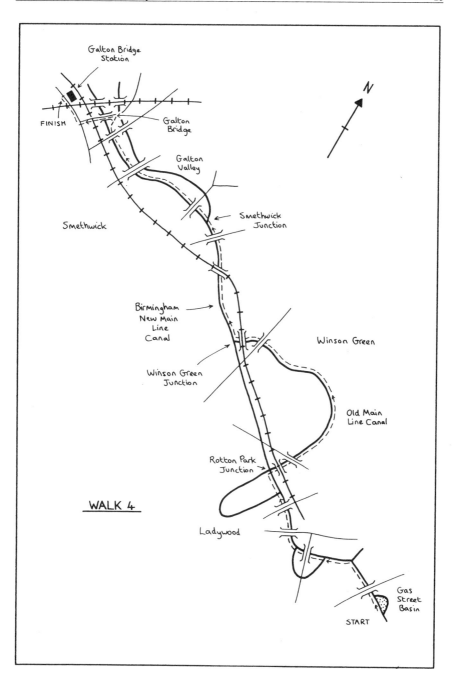

WALK 4

The pumping station at Galton Valley, Smethwick

uses deep cuttings to make its way through the Galton Valley. From here it is easy to appreciate the importance of the Galton Valley as a route centre. Both canals, the railway line between Birmingham and Wolverhampton and two main roads all make their way through it.

E. The cast-iron Galton Bridge, built by Telford in 1829, rises 71 feet (21m) above the canal and is a most impressive sight. It – and indeed the whole area – is named after Samuel Galton (1753-1832), a local industrialist.

# 5. Sutton Park

**Start/Parking:** Sutton Park Visitors Centre, ¼ mile (0.4km) to the west of Town Gate – grid ref. 114963

**Distance:** 3½ miles (5.6km)

**Category:** Easy

**Refreshments:** Light refreshments available in the park

**Terrain:** Mainly on clear and well-surfaced tracks and paths through woodland and across open heathland.

**OS Maps:** Landranger 139, Explorer 220

**Public transport:** Buses from Birmingham city centre, Solihull, Walsall, Tamworth and Lichfield, and trains from Birmingham and Lichfield to Sutton Coldfield town centre; then walk along Park Road to enter Sutton Park via Town Gate

## Discover:

Throughout most of this walk, it is difficult to believe that you are wholly within the boundaries of Britain's second city and but a short distance from housing estates, busy roads and the M6 motorway. Hardly a building can be seen and some of the views are reminiscent of Dartmoor or the lower slopes of the Pennines, especially in late summer and autumn when the heather is out. Although a short walk, it introduces you to the three main features of the park's landscape: woodland, open heathland and the various pools that are scattered around it.

## Route Directions:

Begin by walking along the tarmac track in front of the Visitors Centre (A) to a junction of park roads and drives and keep ahead along the tarmac drive signposted to Keeper's Pool. Follow the drive through trees to a car park and turn right just beyond it to walk across the end of the pool, a very attractive spot. Keep ahead along a path through the woodland of Lower Nut Hurst to Blackroot Pool, (B) continue beside the left edge of the pool but, at a fork a few yards ahead, take the left-hand path, which bears left to a T-junction. Turn left along a broad, gently ascending track which narrows, levels off and continues to a fork. Take the left-hand wider path, into open heathland and across two parallel tarmac drives near where they join. To the right is a plaque which commemorates the World Scout Jamboree held here in 1957.

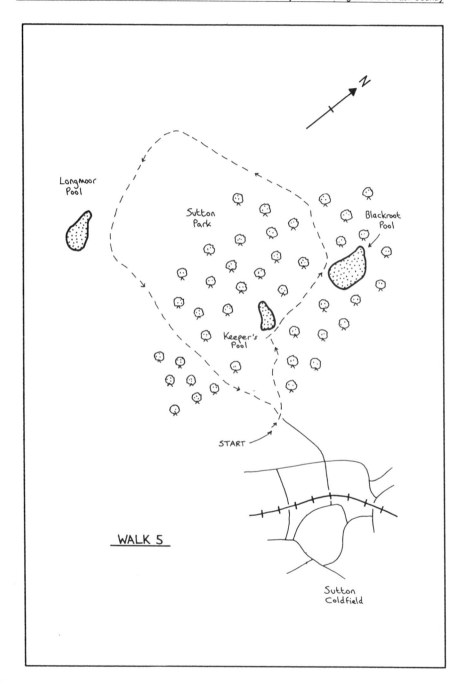

WALK 5

After crossing the drives, keep ahead and just before you start to descend, turn left onto a path and head down to a junction. Take the second path on the left – do not turn sharp left onto the first path – and continue across an open landscape of heather, bracken, gorse and grass. As the path descends, Longmoor Pool can be seen over to the right. At a T-junction, turn left along a tarmac drive, keep ahead at a crossroads and the drive heads gently downhill back to the Visitors Centre.

## Features of Interest:

**A.** For generations, Brummies have been coming to Sutton Park on fine weekends and bank holidays. It was originally an area of wood and rough heathland on the edge of the Royal Forest of Cannock and later became a chase held by the Earls of Warwick. In the 16th century, Bishop Vesey, bishop of Exeter and a local boy made good, persuaded Henry VIII to give it to the people of Sutton Coldfield in perpetuity, hence its survival as a large wedge – nearly 2500 acres – of genuinely open and unspoilt countryside on the edge of Birmingham.

**B.** Keeper's and Blackroot are two of a number of pools in the park which are both attractive landscape features and useful focal points for walkers. Their original purpose was to ensure a regular supply of fish and some of them date back to the 15th century.

Keeper's Pool, Sutton Park

# 6. Valleys of East Birmingham

**Start/Parking:** Kingshurst, Babbs Mill Lake car park off Fordbridge Road – grid ref. 167877

**Finish:** Sheldon Country Park, Church Road entrance – grid ref. 151846

**Distance:** 4½ miles (7.2km)

**Category:** Easy

**Refreshments:** Bell Inn by Bell Lane entrance to Sheldon Country Park, tea-room at Sheldon Country Park

**Terrain:** Paths beside the River Cole and adjacent streams and pools, plus areas of parkland

**OS Maps:** Landranger 139, Explorer 220

**Public transport:** Buses from Birmingham city centre, Solihull and Sutton Coldfield to Fordbridge Road; from there it is a short walk to Babbs Mill Lake

## Discover:

The valleys of the River Cole and some of its tributary streams create attractive and welcome 'green fingers' amidst the post-war housing estates on the eastern fringes of Birmingham and give you some idea of what the area was like before the city's rapid expansion. Two pools further enhance the scene and after a brief stretch beside the perimeter fence of Birmingham Airport, the walk finishes in the pleasant surroundings of Sheldon Country Park by a farm and medieval church, rare features in a modern city suburb.

## Route Directions:

Start by facing the lake (A), turn right and at the far end of the car park, go through a kissing gate and take the tarmac path beside the lake. After passing beside a barrier, turn left to cross a bridge over a brook and continue to the end of the lake.

Cross a footbridge over the River Cole and in front of Babbs Mill Cottage, turn left to pass beside another barrier and walk along the right bank of the river. On reaching a main road, cross over, turn left to recross the river and turn right onto a tarmac path, which runs between Forth Drive on the left and above the Cole on the right. At a T-junction, turn right, in the Alcott Wood and Sheldon direction, to cross the river

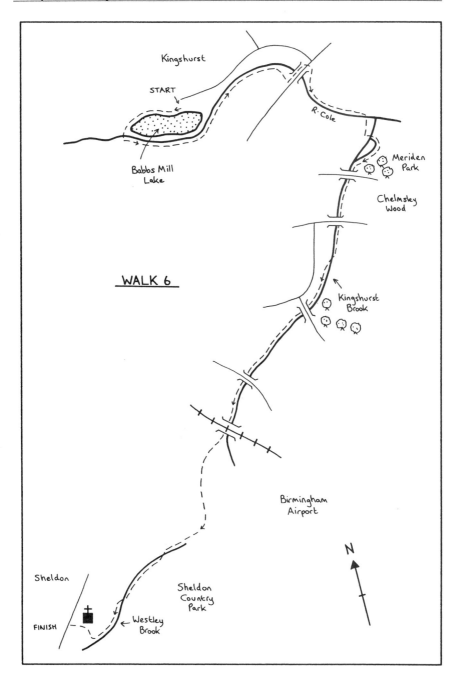

Kingshurst

START

R. Cole

Babbs Mill Lake

Meriden Park

Chelmsley Wood

WALK 6

Kingshurst Brook

Birmingham Airport

N

Sheldon

Sheldon Country Park

FINISH

Westley Brook

for the last time and enter Meriden Park. Keep ahead along a tarmac track and at a junction, turn left to cross a brick bridge over the end of a pool. At a T-junction on the far side, turn right and at the next one, turn right again to walk beside the pool to its far end. Follow the path under a road bridge and continue beside Kingshurst Brook on the right, going under two more road bridges.

Turn right over the first footbridge across the brook after the second road bridge, turn left along a tarmac drive to a road (Bell Lane), cross over and pass beside a barrier to enter Sheldon Country Park. Take the path ahead across a meadow, cross a footbridge and keep ahead to pass under a railway viaduct by Hatchford Brook. Continue across rough meadowland, bear right on joining a wider path and continue alongside the perimeter fence of Birmingham Airport. Cross a footbridge over a brook and at a fork about 20 yards (18m) ahead, take the right-hand path away from the airport fence. Pass through a belt of trees and continue by the left edge of a meadow.

After crossing a footbridge, keep ahead beside Westley Brook on the left and the houses and church tower of Sheldon can be seen in front. Cross a tarmac path, keep ahead, bear left to cross the brook and bear right to continue along its left bank to a T-junction. Turn right to recross the brook, immediately turn left to keep along its right bank again and the path later curves right towards the farm, church and car park.(B) In front of Sheldon church, turn left along a drive to Church Road.

To return to the start, take bus 71 to the junction of Fordbridge Road and Gilson Way and from here continue for a short distance along the road to Babbs Mill Lake car park.

## Features of Interest:

**A.** Babbs Mill Lake is the largest of several pools in the Cole valley. Since 1985 around 7 miles (11.3km) of the valley – between Coventry Road at Hay Mills and the M6 at Chelmsley Wood – has been cared for under Project Kingfisher, a joint scheme between Birmingham and Solihull councils together with the Countryside Commission, English Nature, Environment Agency, Urban Wildlife Trust and Warwickshire Wildlife Trust.

**B.** About 240 acres of grassland, woodland and wetland makes up Sheldon Country Park, a valuable open space sandwiched between Birmingham International Airport and housing estates on the edge of Birmingham and Solihull. Its focal point is Old Rectory Farm, which

The River Cole near Kingshurst

survived the suburban sprawl and has been restored as a working farm. It has a variety of farm animals, some horses and ponies and a cottage garden. To complete this idyllic rural scene, the farm is overlooked by the tower of Sheldon's 14th-century church. Like most of the medieval, former village churches in the suburbs of Birmingham, it was heavily restored in the Victorian era.

# 7. Cole Valley – Sarehole Mill to Trittiford Mill Pool

**Start/Parking:** Sarehole Mill, off Cole Bank Road on the borders of Moseley and Hall Green – grid ref. 099818

**Distance:** 3 miles (4.8km)

**Category:** Easy

**Refreshments:** Sherwood pub and Greenhill Café in Highfield Road

**Terrain:** Mainly through woodland and across meadows bordering a river, plus a circuit of a pool

**OS Maps:** Landranger 139, Explorer 220

**Public transport:** Buses from Birmingham city centre to the junction of Stratford Road and Cole Bank Road, then walk down Cole Bank Road to Sarehole Mill

---

## Discover:

This walk explores a pleasant stretch of the Cole valley, a narrow green finger in south Birmingham, between Sarehole Mill and Trittiford Mill Pool on the borders of Hall Green, Moseley and Yardley Wood. An outward route mostly along the east bank of the river is followed by a circuit of the pool and a return along the west bank. This area of the Cole valley is 'Tolkien country' as the writer spent much of his childhood in the locality, in those days – around the turn of the 20th century – still genuinely rural as Birmingham's suburban expansion did not reach this far until the 1920s.

## Route Directions:

From the car park by Sarehole Mill (A) cross the road, go through a gate opposite and take the tarmac path through a narrow strip of woodland beside the River Cole. At the next road (Brook Lane), a brief detour to the right enables you to view some of the few remaining post-war pre-fabs (B).

Cross the road, keep ahead along Coleside Avenue and just before reaching the end of the road, turn left to cross a brick, four-arched bridge over the river. Turn right to continue across grass through The Dingles and go through a gate onto Highfield Road. The pub and café are

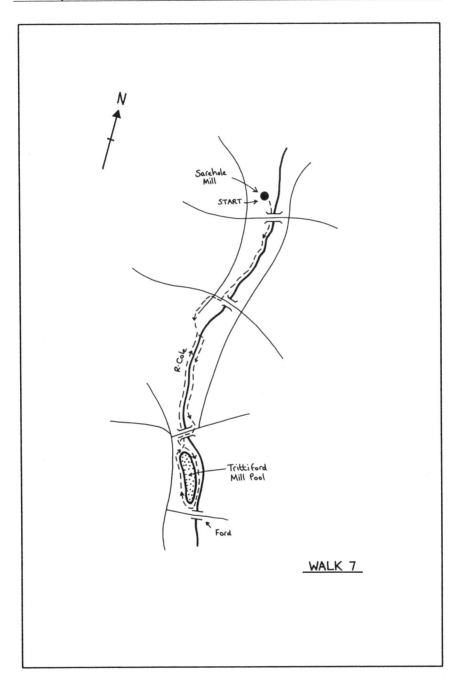

WALK 7

just to the left. Cross the road, turn right to recross the river, immediately turn left onto a worn path across grass to the end of Trittiford Mill Pool and bear left onto the tarmac path which encircles the pool (C). At the far tapering end, turn right to cross a bridge and turn left and left again for another brief detour to the ford in Scribers Lane.

After crossing the bridge, the route continues to the right along the other side of the pool to return to Highfield Road. Cross over, pass through a fence gap and walk back through The Dingles along the opposite bank of the Cole from the outward route, following signs to Sarehole Mill. Initially you walk along a pleasant tree-lined path between the river and a brook but after turning left over a footbridge, you continue along the right edge of a meadow and finally along a tree-lined path again to the end of Coleside Avenue. Here you pick up the outward route and retrace your steps to the start.

## Features of Interest:

**A.** This brick-built, 18th-century, water-powered corn mill is the last one surviving in an area which once had many. J.R.R. Tolkien and his brother used to play in the surrounding meadows and visit the mill when small boys – the family lived here between 1896 and 1900

Sarehole Mill

– and the writer describes the frightening-looking father and son who worked the mill at the time. He loved the countryside of the Cole valley, which was still rural as the city's suburbs did not start to reach out this far until after the First World War.

**B.** The prefabs at the bottom end of Wake Green Road are a rare survival of the many that were put up hurriedly after the end of the Second World War as a way of solving the desperate housing shortage and shortages of building materials at the time.

**C.** As its name suggests, this was one of the many mill pools in the Cole valley but the mill has long since disappeared. Its tree-shaded banks form the focal point of a small but pleasant area of parkland.

# 8. Cannon Hill Park, River Rea and Highbury Park

**Start:** Cannon Hill Park, Edgbaston Road entrance – grid ref. 069841

**Distance:** 3½ miles (5.6km)

**Category:** Easy

**Parking:** There are two car parks in Cannon Hill Park, one off Edgbaston Road and the other off Russell Road

**Refreshments:** Garden Tearoom and Midlands Arts Centre café in Cannon Hill Park, Highbury pub in Moor Green Lane

**Terrain:** Much of the route is on tarmac paths through parkland, with short stretches across grass and through woodland

**OS Maps:** Landranger 139, Explorer 220

**Public transport:** Buses from Birmingham city centre

## Discover:

The grassland, woodland and pools of the adjacent Cannon Hill Park, Holders Lane Woods and Highbury Park, on the borders of Edgbaston, Moseley and King's Heath, form a large green area in the Rea valley amidst the suburbs of south Birmingham. The many fine views across the valley are dominated by the Chamberlain Tower of Birmingham University and the route passes close to Highbury Hall, former home of Joseph Chamberlain.

## Route Directions:

Enter the park (A) and take the wide tarmac track through it, passing the Garden Tearoom and following Rea Valley Cycle Path signs. Shortly after passing the Golden Lion (B) on the right, the track curves right towards a brick bridge over a pool but before reaching it, turns left – now signposted as the Rea Valley Cycle Way and Walkway – to continue beside the River Rea on the right.

At a signpost to the left of a bridge, turn left, in the Moseley direction, turn left again at a T-junction and head gently uphill towards trees. On reaching the top, turn right along an attractive path through the narrow strip of Holders Lane Woods and at a three-way fork, continue along the

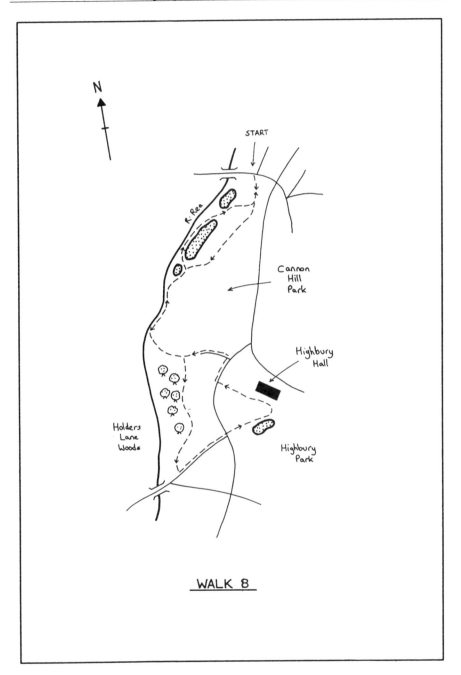

N

START

R. Rea

Cannon
Hill
Park

Highbury
Hall

Holders
Lane
Woods

Highbury
Park

WALK 8

Highbury Hall

middle path which emerges into a meadow. Bear right across it, go through a hedge gap and walk across the next meadow to a tarmac track.

Turn left and pass beside two barriers to reach a road (Moor Green Lane) opposite the Highbury pub. Turn left up to a T-junction where you turn right and almost immediately left onto a tarmac path to enter Highbury Park. At a crossroads about 20 yards (18m) ahead, turn right onto a path which keeps along the left edge of a pool. Just beyond the end of the pool – where the path bears right – turn left and head uphill across grass and through trees. To the right Highbury Hall (C) can be seen through the trees. At the top you join a tarmac track which bears left to a lodge and here you leave the park. Turn right along Moor Green Lane and turn left into Holders Lane, bending right at a T-junction and following Cycle Way signs to Birmingham University, to re-enter Holders Lane Woods. Here you rejoin the outward route and retrace your steps to the brick bridge near the end of the pool in Cannon Hill Park.

For an alternative finale, turn left over the bridge and then turn right to walk alongside the pool. Just after passing the Midland Arts Centre, continue along the right edge of the next pool but at a fork, take the right-hand path which veers away from it. Pass to the right of a Boer

War memorial and turn right at a crossroads of paths to a T-junction in front of the Garden Tearoom. Turn left onto the Cycle Way to return to the start.

## Features of Interest:

A. Cannon Hill Park, Birmingham's premier park, comprises around 80 acres of formal parkland, plus an adjoining 120 acres of wetland, meadow and woodland. It was formerly the estate of the Ryland family and after being donated to the people of Birmingham in 1873, the Rylands financed a landscaping programme, which included the construction of pools and the planting of ornamental gardens. Nowadays there are children's play areas and sporting and leisure facilities and within the confines of the park are the Birmingham Nature Centre and Midlands Arts Centre.

B. The half-timbered Golden Lion Inn originally stood in Deritend in the centre of Birmingham and was re-erected here in 1911 to avoid demolition. It dates from the 17th century and formerly belonged to the Guild of St John the Baptist at Deritend.

C. Highbury Hall was built by Joseph Chamberlain in 1880 and was his home until his death in 1914. He named it after the area of London in which he previously lived.

# 9. King's Norton

**Start:** King's Norton, The Green – grid ref. 049789

**Distance:** 3½ miles (5.6km)

**Category:** Easy

**Parking:** Around The Green at King's Norton

**Refreshments:** Bulls Head and Manteli's Coffee Shop at The Green

**Terrain:** Flat route, mostly along canal towpaths

**OS Maps:** Landranger 139, Explorer 220

**Public transport:** Buses from Birmingham city centre, Bromsgrove, Evesham and Redditch

## Discover:

Perhaps the most surprising discovery on this short walk is The Green at King's Norton, a genuine village green, complete with pub and medieval church, amidst the suburbs of Birmingham. Most of the route is along pleasant, peaceful and leafy stretches of the Worcester and Birmingham and Stratford-upon-Avon canals – which meet at King's Norton Junction – passing some interesting canal architecture.

## Route Directions:

Start by walking down to the main road (A) and at a roundabout, take the second road on the right (Masshouse Lane). Where the road bears left to cross a canal bridge, descend steps and turn left along the towpath of the Worcester and Birmingham Canal (B). By the toll house at King's Norton Junction (C), turn right over a brick bridge (no 72) and continue by the Stratford-upon-Avon Canal, passing a Guillotine Lock and Swing Bridge, as far as the entrance to Brandwood Tunnel (322m) (D). From here retrace your steps to King's Norton Junction, recross the brick bridge, turn left and immediately bear right onto a path, signposted 'Rea Valley Route, King's Norton'. As you follow this path across fields to the main road, there is a fine view ahead of the tower and spire of King's Norton church.

At the main road, turn left and just after passing King's Norton Library, turn right along a tree-lined track towards the church. Turn left

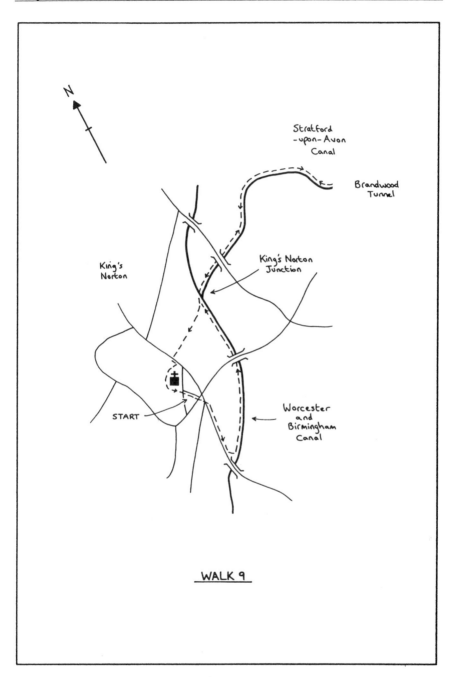

Stratford
-upon-Avon
Canal

Brandwood
Tunnel

King's Norton
Junction

King's
Norton

Worcester
and
Birmingham
Canal

START

WALK 9

through the churchyard, passing in front of the church, to return to The Green.

## Features of Interest:

**A.** There is probably more of a village atmosphere at The Green in King's Norton than anywhere else in Birmingham. Around the tree-shaded, triangular green are attractive old buildings, including the medieval church, pub and a timber-framed former grammar school. The church, with its lofty 15th-century tower and spire, dominates this deceptively rural scene.

Stop lock, King's Norton

**B.** For details of the Worcester and Birmingham Canal, see Walk 3.

**C.** Constructed in the early 19th century, the Stratford-upon-Avon canal runs from King's Norton Junction to where it empties into the River Avon by the Royal Shakespeare Theatre at Stratford. The Junction House, built in 1802, was a toll-house and traffic passing from one canal to the other had to stop here in order to be gauged and pay the appropriate toll. A little way along the Stratford Canal is the unusual Guillotine Lock, also constructed in 1802. This controlled the flow of water between the two canals and gets its name because the gates were suspended in iron frames by chains.

**D.** The Brandwood Tunnel, which has an impressive brick portal, is 352 yards (325m) long. There is no towing path through it.

# 10. Woodgate Valley and Harborne

**Start/Parking:** Woodgate Valley Country Park, Clapgate Lane – grid ref. 995829

**Finish:** Harborne, High Street – grid ref. 030844

**Distance:** 3½ miles (5.6km)

**Category:** Easy

**Refreshments:** Tearoom at Woodgate Valley Country Park Visitors Centre, Hillyfields pub at junction of Quinton Road and Grove Lane, pubs and cafés at Harborne

**Terrain:** Clear paths through a country park and beside a stream, followed by pleasant walking along quiet suburban roads

**OS Maps:** Landranger 139, Explorers 219 and 220

**Public transport:** Buses from Birmingham city centre

## Discover:

Most of the route is through an area of parkland that forms an attractive 'green wedge' amidst the south-western suburbs of Birmingham. As much of it is beside Bourn Brook, this makes route finding relatively easy. The rural nature of the walk is further emphasised by the combination of medieval church and old pub at Harborne, one of the city's most attractive suburbs that manages to retain a village atmosphere.

## Route Directions:

Begin by walking along the tarmac path to the left of the Visitors Centre (A), continue along a fence-lined path and descend gently to reach a well-surfaced path in front of a footbridge over Bourn Brook. Turn right onto the path and keep beside the meandering brook to emerge, via a fence gap, onto a road (West Boulevard).

Cross carefully, keep ahead along a tarmac path and then across grass to rejoin the brook and turn right to continue along an attractive grassy path beside it. At the next road (California Way), cross over into Stonehouse Hill but immediately turn left to walk along another grassy path by the right bank of Bourn Brook. After crossing stepping stones over the brook, continue along its left bank. Keep ahead at the first footbridge but at the next one, turn left along a tarmac path up to a main

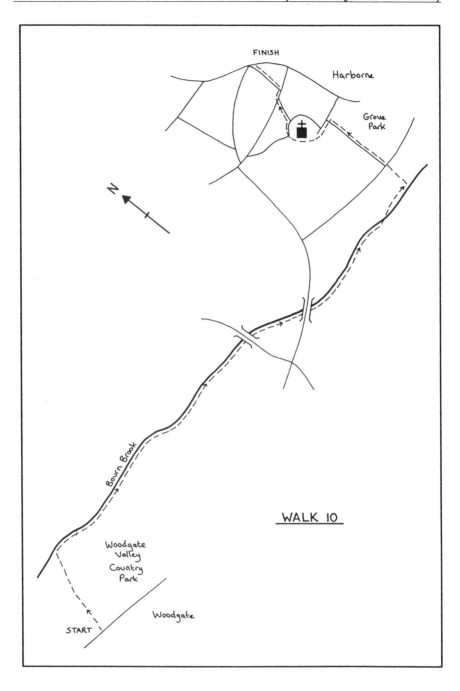

road (Quinton Road). Cross over, keep ahead along Grove Lane, passing along the left edge of the attractive Grove Park, and turn left at a T-junction. Where the road bends right, keep ahead into Harborne churchyard, pass to the left of the church, turn right in front of it and turn left to emerge onto a road by the Bell Inn (B). Turn right along Old Church Road, take the first turning on the left (St Peter's Road) and turn left along Albert Road into the centre of Harborne.

From here bus 23 will return you to the entrance to Woodgate Valley Country Park.

## Features of Interest:

**A.** Woodgate Valley Country Park comprises 450 acres of meadows, woods and streams near the south western edge of Birmingham and on the fringes of the Black Country. From many points in the park there are fine views across the valley of Bourn Brook. Near the Visitors Centre there is an urban farm, with several rare or unusual breeds of animals.

**B.** Pub, bowling green and medieval church create a real village atmosphere at Harborne, especially on a fine summer day when people

Woodgate Valley Country Park

are sitting outside the pub. The church has a 15th-century tower but the rest was mainly rebuilt in 1867. David Cox, a noted Victorian landscape painter, is buried in the churchyard and Elihu Burritt, American consul in Birmingham in the 1860s and author of 'Walks in the Black Country and Its Green Border-Land', chose to live in Harborne which was still very rural at the time. He desribes the congregation coming 'across the broad fields that converge from every direction into the solemn aisles of the churchyard trees'.

# 11. Barr Beacon and the Rushall Canal

**Start/Parking:** Barr Beacon, Monument car park – grid ref. 061973

**Distance:** 8 miles (12.9km)

**Category:** Moderate

**Refreshments:** None

**Terrain:** Open hillside and woodland with a lengthy middle section along a canal towpath

**OS Maps:** Landranger 139, Explorer 220

**Public transport:** Buses from Walsall and Great Barr

## Discover:

The superb viewpoint of Barr Beacon stands at a height of 744 feet (227m) above a substantial wedge of open country lying between Birmingham and Walsall. From here the route descends across fields and along a tree-lined drive to Great Barr church and then on to the towpath of the Rushall Canal. A 2½ mile (4km) stretch beside the canal is followed by some attractive woodland walking before a fairly easy and gentle ascent returns you to the start. Much of the walk is along the well-waymarked Beacon Way.

## Route Directions:

Begin by the war memorial and cross the tarmac drive to a Beacon Way sign. Turn left and follow a path, between gorse bushes and across the open grassland of the hill (A), descending to a road. Cross over and take the path ahead through Beacon Spinney, continuing to descend and bearing left at a waymarked post to a stile. Climb it, descend steps to a fork and take the right-hand path, which keeps below the face of Beacon Quarry. At the next fork, take the right-hand path again, climb a stile onto a road, cross over and continue along a path that keeps parallel to the road opposite. After following the road around a left bend, continue first along the verge on the right, then along an enclosed path and finally along the road itself to Great Barr's 19th-century church. Just beyond the church, bear right through a kissing gate and walk along a

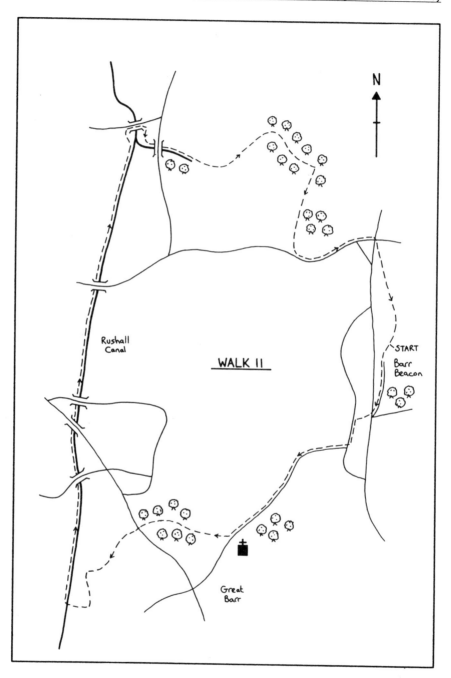

straight, tree-lined drive through Merrions Wood, laid out by Sir Joseph Scott in 1797 and landscaped by Humphrey Repton. Look out for where a Beacon Way sign directs you to turn left onto a path which winds through trees and at a fork, take the right-hand path which emerges, via a stile, onto the busy A34.

Cross carefully and head through a car park and across grass to the next Beacon Way sign. Keep ahead to the next one where you bear left through a narrow belt of trees and walk along the left edge of Aston University playing fields. The route continues first along an enclosed path and then along the edge of the playing fields again to a footbridge in the field corner. Cross it, turn left along the left edge of the next field and about 100 yards (91m) before the corner, turn right onto a clear worn path which heads across the field. On the far side bear right along an enclosed path, cross a canal bridge, turn sharp left down to the canal and turn left again to pass under the bridge. You now continue along the towpath of the Rushall Canal for the next 2½ miles (4km) (B). On reaching Longwood Junction – just after passing the second flight of locks, the Rushall Flight – turn left up to a road and then turn right to cross Longwood Bridge. Turn right along a lane, cross a road and take the tarmac track ahead into Hayhead Wood Local Nature Reserve (C). The track bends first right, then left and where it bends sharply right again, keep ahead to a Beacon Way post and follow the path to the right into woodland. Turn left at a T-junction in front of a pool, turn right at the next T-junction and at the next one a few yards ahead, turn left. At a fork take the left-hand path and at a T-junction near the edge of the trees, turn right along the left inside edge of woodland. Turn left to cross a plank footbridge, continue along an enclosed path, cross a footbridge over a brook and keep ahead. At a waymark, turn left down steps, cross another footbridge and continue along an enclosed path.

The path turns right over another footbridge and continues into trees to a T-junction. Turn left and keep through a narrow strip of woodland – there are steps and footbridges in places – looking out for the regular Beacon Way signs and curving right to eventually reach a stile on the far edge of Cuckoo Nook. Climb the stile, walk along an enclosed path, by a line of trees on the left, continue along the left edge of fields and climb a stile onto a road. Turn left up to a crossroads, cross over and at the next Beacon Way sign, turn right and pass through a hedge gap. Continue across the grassy and gorse-strewn slopes, making for a barrier, pass beside it and walk along a tarmac path alongside a reservoir embankment on the right. After passing beside another barrier, the path curves right to return to the start.

## Features of Interest:

**A.** For many centuries beacons have been lit on Barr Beacon at times of national celebration, such as the defeat of the Spanish Armada in 1588, and it is one of the finest viewpoints and most prominent landmarks in the Midlands. The Monument was erected in the 1930s both in memory of Colonel Wilkinson, who gave this site to the public in 1919, and as a war memorial.

Barr Beacon

**B.** The Rushall Canal was completed in 1847, making it one of the latest canals to be built. It linked the Tame Valley Canal with the Anglesey Branch of the Wyrley and Essington Canal, thus opening up a more direct route between Birmingham and the expanding coalfields in the Cannock area at the time.

**C.** Hayhead Wood Nature Reserve has been reclaimed from an area formerly mined for limestone for use in the iron smelting industries of the Black Country.

# 12. Sandwell Valley Country Park

**Start/Parking:** Sandwell Valley Country Park, Sandwell Park Farm, sign-posted from A41 and West Bromwich town centre – grid ref. 018913

**Distance:** 4 miles (6.4km)

**Category:** Easy

**Refreshments:** Tearoom at Sandwell Park Farm

**Terrain:** Generally flat going, mainly through woodland and across parkland, with some riverside and lakeside walking

**OS Maps:** Landranger 139, Explorer 220

**Public transport:** None

## Discover:

Despite being sandwiched between West Bromwich and the north western suburbs of Birmingham and bisected by the M5, this is an attractive rural walk with fine stretches of woodland, a pleasant lakeside stroll and views across the Tame valley. There is also the opportunity to visit two farms and the route passes near a nature reserve and by the scanty remains of a small medieval priory.

## Route Directions:

In the car park (A) go through a kissing gate, at a Beacon Way sign, and walk along a winding, fence-lined path through trees, crossing several footbridges, to a T-junction. Turn right, climb steps and turn left onto a tarmac track to cross a footbridge over the M5. Keep ahead – the track soon becomes a rough one – to reach the fragmentary remains of Sandwell Priory (B). Continue through woodland to a lane, cross over and keep ahead along the tree-lined path opposite. Just before reaching houses on the edge of Birmingham, turn left onto a path which heads gently uphill across open grassland to a World War II gun emplacement on a low brow. Here you pick up a concrete path and follow it into woodland to a crossroads. Turn left and on reaching a gap in the trees on the right, turn right and head gently downhill across fields to emerge onto a tarmac drive.

    Turn right and in front of the entrance to Park Farm, bear left onto a path, which runs between two golf courses, curving gently downhill to

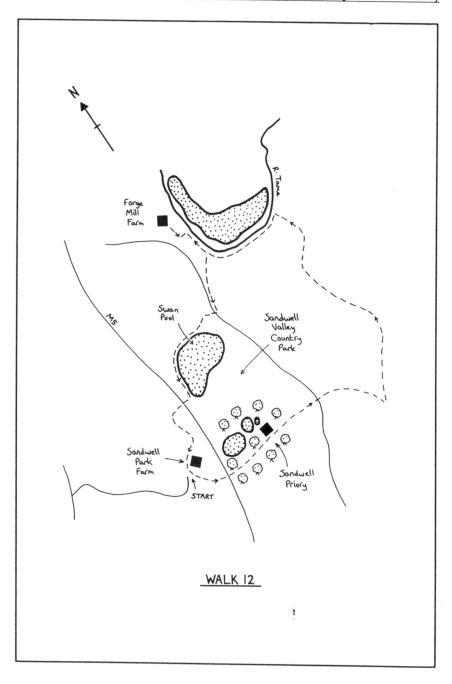

N

R. Tame

Forge
Mill
Farm

Swan
Pool

Sandwell
Valley
Country
Park

M5

Sandwell
Park
Farm

Sandwell
Priory

START

WALK 12

the River Tame. Turn left along the embankment above the river and follow it around a right bend to a T-junction.

If you wish to visit Forge Mill Farm (C), turn right – there is a fine view to the right over the pool -and then turn left and right again to reach the farm.

At the T-junction the main route continues to the left along a well-surfaced track, part of both the Beacon Way and a National Cycle Route. Follow this curving track to a lane, cross over and take the path opposite, which bends right to a track. Turn left, passing to the right of the Sandwell Valley Sailing Centre, bear left to Swan Pool and turn right onto a tarmac track beside it. Follow the curve of the pool to the left and at a crossroads by the corner of the pool, turn right and to re-cross the M5 by a footbridge. About 100 yards (91m) beyond the bridge, turn left through a kissing gate onto a path and at a fence corner, turn left to keep alongside the fence. On reaching a tarmac drive, turn left and follow the curve of the drive to the right, passing the buildings of Sandwell Park Farm, to return to the start.

Sandwell Park Farm

# Features of Interest:

**A.** The country park was part of the estate of the Earls of Dartmouth and Sandwell Park Farm was the home farm for the estate. Built in the reign of Queen Anne, it is now a Victorian working farm, employing machines and methods used in the late 19$^{th}$ century. It also serves as a Visitor Centre for the country park and there is a walled garden, Victorian street scene, together with displays and finds detailing the history of the nearby priory.

**B.** Sandwell Priory, a small and rather poor Benedictine monastery, was founded in the 12th century. After it was dissolved by Henry VIII, a house was built on the site and in the 18th century this was replaced by the fine mansion of Sandwell Hall, the residence of the Earls of Dartmouth. The demolition of the hall in 1928 revealed some of the foundations of the medieval priory and the site was excavated in the 1980s.

**C.** As the name suggests, Forge Mill Farm is built on the site of a 16$^{th}$-century water-powered iron forge. It is now a modern dairy farm and has a visitor centre, shop and farm trail. On the other side of the pool there is a RSPB nature reserve, created in 1982 near the site of the former Hamstead colliery.

# 13. Hawne Basin and Leasowes Park

**Start/Parking:** Leasowes Park, off A458 (Birmingham-Stourbridge road) near the bottom of Mucklow Hill – grid ref. 975842

**Distance:** 2½ miles (4km)

**Category:** Easy

**Refreshments:** None

**Terrain:** Two brief stretches along a canal towpath; most of the remainder is along clear paths through well-wooded parkland

**OS Maps:** Landranger 139, Explorer 219

**Public transport:** Buses from Birmingham, Halesowen and Kidderminster

## Discover:

After a brief initial walk beside the Dudley No 2 Canal by Hawne Basin, the remainder of the route is through woods, beside streams and alongside pools in Leasowes Park, beautifully landscaped in the 18th century and of tremendous historic interest. At various points, there are impressive views looking across the nearby town of Halesowen to the Clent Hills.

## Route Directions:

With your back to the canal, take the tarmac track to the left of the Wardens Base building and at a T-junction in front of houses, turn left along an uphill, hedge-lined track. Continue along a road to the main road, turn left, then turn right to cross at traffic lights and keep ahead downhill along a tarmac drive towards an industrial estate.

At a fork, take the right-hand track which curves right below an embankment to a public footpath sign to Gorsty Hill and from here you continue down to the Dudley No 2 Canal opposite Hawne Basin (A). Keep beside the canal as far as a footbridge (Coombes Bridge), turn right up steps and continue across the open grassland of Coombeswood. Cross a track and continue steadily uphill along an enclosed path, climbing two stiles and turning right over a third one. To the right is a fine view over Halesowen to the Clent Hills. After climbing another stile, keep ahead to the main road again.

Cross it, turn left and after about 50 yards (46m), turn right over a

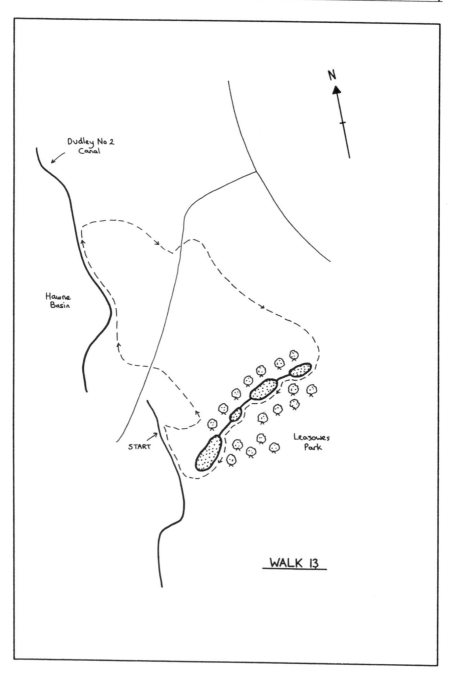

N

Dudley No 2
Canal

Hawne
Basin

START

Leasowes
Park

WALK 13

stile to re-enter Leasowes Park (B). Keep by a hedge on the right, then cross part of a golf course into trees, go through a hedge gap and turn right alongside an iron fence on the right. Continue along the bottom right-hand edge of a sloping field, descend gently into woodland and follow the path to the right, keeping above a stream on the left. Cross a track, keep ahead and bear left to cross a footbridge over the stream by Beech Water. Turn right and the path curves sharply to the left, then turns right over another footbridge and right again alongside the pool. At the end of the pool, cross a tarmac track and continue through more beautiful woodland – now with the stream on the right – descending gently all the while and crossing the stream three times in quick succession. Keep ahead – the stream is now on the left – cross another track, head downhill and recross the stream once more. After climbing steps, continue along to the delightful Priory Pool (or Breaches Pool) and at a T-junction by the corner of the pool, turn right over a footbridge.

Turn right again to walk beside the pool, climb a flight of steps at the far end and at the top, turn right alongside the Dudley No 2 Canal. To the left is a grand view of the tower of Halesowen's Norman church backed by the Clent Hills. A short walk by the canal leads back to the start.

## Features of Interest:

**A.** Now a marina, Hawne Basin was opened in 1797 as a commercial wharf serving Halesowen. Dudley No 2 Canal, begun in 1793, was built to provide a link between Dudley No 1 Canal and the Worcester and Birmingham Canal at Selly Oak. From Hawne Basin southwards it has been filled in, apart from a short isolated stretch alongside Leasowes Park which is managed by the Lapal Canal Trust.

**B.** In the 18th century, Leasowes Park was one of the most visited gardens in the country and its survival is little short of miraculous, on the edge of Birmingham and the Black Country, sandwiched between busy main roads and only a stone's throw from the M5. It was inherited in 1742 as a working farm by the poet William Shenstone and, over the following years, he re-designed it, not in the contemporary formal style but on natural lines. He planted areas of woodland, created grassy glades and built cascades and pools, making full use of the hilly terrain. In order to further enhance its 'picturesque' qualities, Shenstone provided several urns and seats at particularly fine viewpoints – looking towards Halesowen church,

Leasowes Park

the Clent Hills or the ruins of Halesowen Abbey – and even constructed the mock ruins of a medieval priory, allegedly taking stones from the nearby abbey. As one of the earliest natural landscape gardens in England, The Leasowes is of considerable historic and landscape value. After Shenstone's death in 1763, the garden was neglected, became overgrown and fell into disrepair but Dudley Council is currently working to restore it to something like its former glory, although subsequent developments – notably the construction of the canal embankment – have destroyed for ever some of the poet's favourite views.

# 14. Saltwells Wood and Mushroom Green

**Start/Parking:** Saltwells Nature Reserve, Saltwells Lane, signposted from Coppice Lane which is off the A4036 between Quarry Bank and Merry Hill – grid ref. 934869

**Distance:** 2½ miles (4km)

**Category:** Easy

**Refreshments:** Saltwells Inn next to car park

**Terrain:** Mainly woodland paths and tracks with no gradients

**OS Maps:** Landranger 139, Explorer 219

**Public transport:** Buses from Birmingham, Redditch, Halesowen, Dudley, Stourbridge and Wolverhampton pass the end of Saltwells Lane

## Discover:

This is a short figure of eight walk through part of the Saltwells Local Nature Reserve, a wedge of open country sandwiched between Dudley, Brierley Hill, Quarry Bank and Cradley Heath. The first half is through the beautiful Saltwells Wood; the second half extends southwards into the chainmakers' hamlet of Mushroom Green. There is a multitude of paths through the wood and the route directions need to be followed carefully but if you did happen to stray from the recommended route, you would not be lost for long in such a compact area surrounded by roads and houses.

## Route Directions:

Begin by passing beside the gate at the far end of the car park, pass beside a barrier by another gate and keep ahead along a path into Saltwells Wood (A). At a five-way junction, keep straight ahead and about 100 yards (91m) before emerging from the trees to reach a stile, turn right up steps and follow a winding path to a T-junction. Turn left, pass beside a gate onto a tarmac drive, bear left along it and after 50 yards (46m), turn right onto another path. On entering a small clearing, the path curves right to a fork where you take the take the left-hand path – there is a wire fence on the left – to meet a well-surfaced path. Turn right along it, bear left on joining another path and at the three-way junction immediately ahead, take the left-hand path.

The path continues along the left inside edge of trees and across the

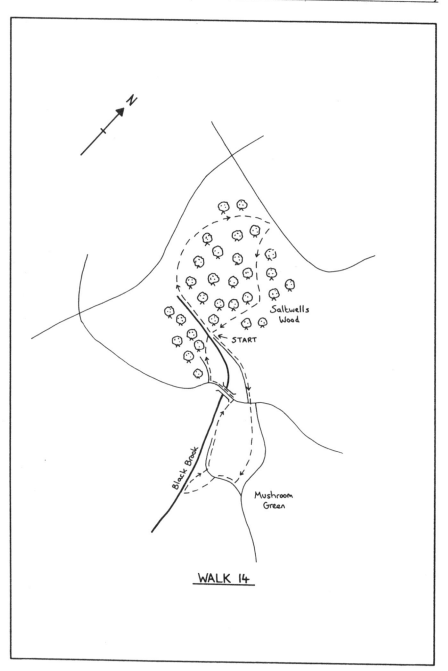

N

Saltwells
Wood

START

Black Brook

Mushroom
Green

WALK 14

The chainmakers' hamlet of Mushroom Green

field on the left, Netherton church can be seen crowning a steep hill. Head downhill to a T-junction, turn right and the path curves left on joining another path to reach the five-way junction passed just after the start of the walk. Turn left to retrace your steps to the car park and continue along Saltwells Lane to the main road.

Cross over, pass beside the fence opposite and walk along the attractive tree- and hedge-lined path ahead (B) into the chainmakers' hamlet of Mushroom Green. On reaching a lane, turn right through the hamlet (C) and look out for where you turn left beside a barrier in order to make a brief detour along a path which descends through woodland to the bridge over Black Brook, a pleasant spot. After returning to Mushroom Green, turn left to continue along the lane which bends right, peters out at the last house and continues as a wooded path along the side of the valley to the main road.

Turn left, follow the road around a left bend and take the first lane on the right. Where the lane bears slightly left, turn right through a fence gap and follow a path through woodland. Cross a bridge over Black Brook, climb steps up to a lane by the Saltwells Inn and turn right to return to the start.

## Features of Interest:

**A.** Saltwells Wood is the oldest established part of the Saltwells Local Nature Reserve, designated in 1981. Originally part of Pensnett Chase, the main part of it was planted by Lady Dudley in 1795 to hide the scars caused by coal mining in the Black Brook valley. Nowadays it comprises mainly oak, beech and sycamore woodland.

**B.** The path follows the track of a former railway, originally built in 1853 to transport coal from the Earl of Dudley's mines in the area. It later carried passengers but was closed in 1945.

**C.** Looking more like a rural village than an industrial hamlet, Mushroom Green housed miners and nailmakers as well as chainmakers. It is probably the best place in the Black Country to appreciate what much of the area would have looked like in the early stages of the Industrial Revolution, before the urban sprawl of the later Victorian period obliterated most of the countryside. There is a restored chainshop here which is an outpost of the Black Country Museum; details of opening times and demonstrations of chainmaking can be obtained from the museum.

# 15. Rowley Hills and Bumble Hole

**Start/Parking:** Warrens Hall Country Park, Rowley Regis, off B4171 between Blackheath and Dudley – grid ref. 956885

**Distance:** 3½ miles (5.6km)

**Category:** Moderate

**Refreshments:** Wheatsheaf and Rowley Olympic at the top of the Rowley Hills, Hailstone and Cock Inn at Springfield, Dry Dock and Wheatsheaf at Windmill End

**Terrain:** One fairly easy climb and descent followed by level walking along a canal towpath

**OS Maps:** Landranger 139, Explorer 219

**Public transport:** Buses from Birmingham, Halesowen and Dudley

## Discover:

The first half of the walk is over the Rowley Hills that lie between Dudley, Netherton, Blackheath and Oldbury. They rise to 876 feet (267m) and provide extensive views across the Black Country to Cannock Chase, Barr Beacon and the Clent Hills. After descending from the hills, the route continues along the towpath of the Dudley No 2 Canal, passing through the Bumble Hole conservation area, formerly an industrial site but now a reclaimed and attractive green area with considerable appeal to anyone interested in industrial archaeology.

## Route Directions:

Begin by facing the main road and take the fence-lined path to the left, which runs roughly parallel to the road and descends to a stile. Climb it, turn right along a minor road up to the main road, turn left and almost immediately turn right to cross the road and walk along a fence-lined path to a stile.

After climbing it, continue along a steadily ascending path over the Rowley Hills (A), first passing through a belt of trees, then keeping by a hedge on the left and later passing to the right of a pool. About 50 yards (46m) before reaching some stables, bear right onto a path up to a T-junction and turn right along a track. At a post, turn left along an

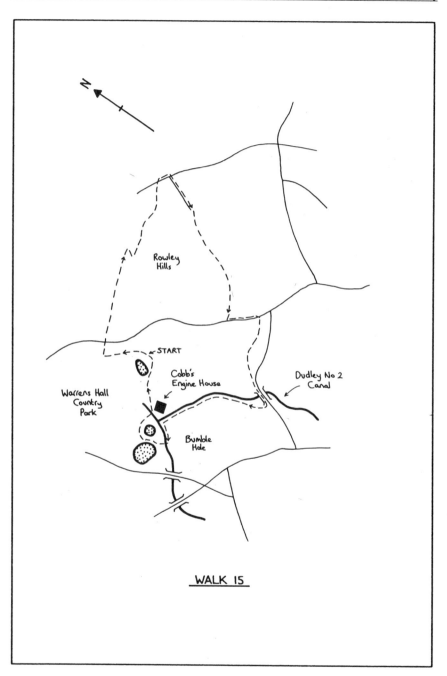

WALK 15

uphill path, pass through a hedge gap and bear left across rough grassland, making for the left edge of a disused quarry.

After bearing right around the edge of the quarry, follow a series of
yellow-topped posts across part of Dudley golf course and on the far
side keep ahead to a road. Turn right along Oakham Road and turn right
again along a lane that bisects two pubs – the Wheatsheaf and Rowley
Olympic. When roughly in line with the radio masts that occupy the
highest point on the Rowley Hills, turn right over a stile, at a public footpath sign, onto the golf course again.

Follow another line of yellow-topped posts to pick up a clear path
which winds downhill – the huge Hailstone Quarry is over to the left
beyond a fence – to a stile. On this descent, there are superb views over
the Black Country to the distinctive outline of the Clent Hills on the
horizon. After climbing the stile, continue downhill, by a fence on the
right, climbing two more stiles, and keep ahead along an enclosed path
to the main road in Springfield. Turn left, passing the Hailstone pub,
and just after Knowle Methodist church – and just before the Cock Inn –
turn right along a downhill path which continues between school
buildings. Turn right and then left to head down to a road and turn right
to continue down to a canal bridge. After crossing it, immediately turn
sharp left to the towpath and pass under the bridge.

Keep beside the Dudley No 2 Canal (B) to the second bridge – to the
left of the prominent landmark of Cobb's Engine House – where you
ascend steps to the left of the bridge and turn left to continue beside the
canal through the Bumble Hole conservation area at Windmill End (C).
Turn right over the first footbridge and turn right again – not beside the
canal but along a path, which initially runs roughly parallel to it and
then bears left across grassland. After passing to the right of a pool, the
path curves right to a T-junction. Turn left, turn right at the next
T-junction and keep ahead towards Cobb's Engine House again.

Re-cross the canal – to the left is the entrance to the Netherton
Tunnel – and turn left to pass to the left of the engine house (D). Continue along an uphill path, take the right-hand path at a fork by a small
pool on the right, and head up to a crossroads. Turn right onto a
well-surfaced path which curves left and keeps along the right edge of
another pool. Bear left on joining a track and pass beside a metal gate to
return to the car park (E).

## Features of Interest:

**A.** The Rowley Hills comprise two main summits – Darby's Hill and Turner's Hill – and rise to 876 feet (267m) above the Black Country. In the past the hills were extensively quarried for their durable rock, known locally as Rowley Rag, which was much used for road surfacing. The vast Hailstone Quarry is passed on the descent.

**B.** For details of Dudley No 2 Canal see Walk 13.

Bumble Hole and Cobb's Engine House

**C.** Bumble Hole is a former area of mining and manufacturing by the junction of the Dudley No 2 and Netherton canals. One theory about its unusual name is that it comes from the noise – *bum-hul* – made by a steam hammer installed in a building at the bottom of a pit, hence 'bum-hul in the hole'. It has been made a conservation area in order to preserve and enhance its industrial heritage and the combination of the cast iron bridges, canal junction, entrance to the Netherton Tunnel, pools reclaimed from industrial dereliction and the abandoned engine house creates an exceptionally attractive and atmospheric spot. There is a Visitors Centre beside the canal.

**D.** The Netherton Tunnel, built between 1855 and 1858, was the last great tunnel of the canal era. It is 3027 feet (2768m) long and stretches from here to the Birmingham Main Line Canal at Dudley Port. Cobb's Engine House near the tunnel entrance, named after a local farmer, was built in 1831 and ceased working in 1928. Inside was a Watt Beam Engine which pumped water out of the local mines.

**E.** Like the adjacent Bumble Hole, Warrens Hall Country Park is a former industrial area – comprising coal mines, brick kilns and boiler works – that has been landscaped and made into attractive green parkland. The spoil heaps of two of the collieries can still be seen.

# 16. Dudley and Wren's Nest

**Start:** Dudley, by the Fountain in High Street – grid ref. 945903

**Distance:** 5½ miles (8.9km)

**Category:** Moderate

**Parking:** Dudley

**Refreshments:** Pubs and cafés at Dudley, Caves pub by Mons Hill

**Terrain:** Parkland and woodland, with some modest climbing over Wren's Nest and Mons Hill

**OS Maps:** Landranger 139, Explorer 219

**Public transport:** Buses from all the surrounding towns

## Discover:

This is a walk full of interest and it is surprising how quickly and easily you emerge into secluded and well-wooded countryside from the busy streets of Dudley. Starting in the town centre, by the zoo and hilltop castle, the route proceeds, via priory ruins and a canal basin, to Wren's Nest National Nature Reserve, a wooded limestone hill, formerly quarried and renowned for its fossils and geological significance. From both Wren's Nest and the neighbouring Mons Hill, there are fine and extensive views to enjoy before returning to the start.

## Route Directions:

Begin in High Street by the elaborate Fountain (A). Nearby is the statue to Duncan Edwards, a native of Dudley and one of the 'Busby Babes' killed in the tragic Manchester United air crash at Munich in 1958. Walk towards the castle and the brick-built, late 18th-century church of St Edmund King and Martyr and turn left down Broadway.

After passing the buildings of Dudley College, turn right into Paganel Drive. Just after passing Gervase Drive, bear left onto a tarmac path that heads across parkland, passing to the right of the ruins of Dudley Priory (B). The path continues through a rose garden and heads gently downhill, alongside a hedge and trees on the right, to a road (Woodland Avenue). Turn right, cross Paganel Drive and at the next road, keep ahead along a path into woodland at the base of Castle Hill. After climbing a stile, turn left along a track through the trees, cross one track and keep ahead to the next one by the Canal Basin, a brief detour to the right (C). Keep ahead along an undulating path - there are steps in places - turning left at a T-junction and later bending right to emerge onto Castle Mill Road.

Turn left, cross a main road, keep ahead along Bluebell Road and then, after a few yards, turn right up steps and follow a path across grass and through trees. Keep ahead at a crossroads and pass through a kissing gate to enter the Wren's Nest National Nature Reserve (D). Turn left, keep along the main path - ignoring all side turns - bear right to pass beside a metal barrier and continue along the left inside edge of the trees. At a fence corner on the left, turn right and head uphill to a crossroads. Turn right and after about 50 yards (46m), turn left to climb a long flight of steps, the '99 Steps'. From the top there is a superb view over Dudley, with the castle ruins standing out prominently.

Continue along a wooded path, which curves left and then bears right to keep by an iron fence bordering the Seven Sisters Quarry. From a viewing platform, you can see the caverns at the base of the quarry face. The path later descends and at the top of more steps, turn left and descend them to view the geological formation of the Ripple Beds, so called from the ripple marks on the rocks made by an ancient sea. At the bottom, turn right along a path that runs along the base of the rock face and emerges, via a kissing gate, onto a road.

Cross over, pass beside a metal gate opposite and follow a narrower path gently downhill through the delightful woodland of Mons Hill (E), still part of the nature reserve. At a fork, take the right-hand path, which heads gently uphill and curves right to a T-junction. Turn right up steps, continue uphill over Mons Hill and then the path descends to a road. Turn left, turn right over a stile and continue along the left inside edge of woodland.

After climbing a metal stile, keep ahead to pass the end of a road, climb another metal stile and continue through the trees as far as a kissing gate on the left. Go through it, here rejoining the outward route, and retrace your steps to Dudley town centre.

## Features of Interest:

**A.** Dudley, 'capital of the Black Country', is a hilltop town dominated by the ruins of a medieval castle, an indication that, unlike most of the other towns and villages in the locality, it was a place of some importance long before the onset of the Industrial Revolution.

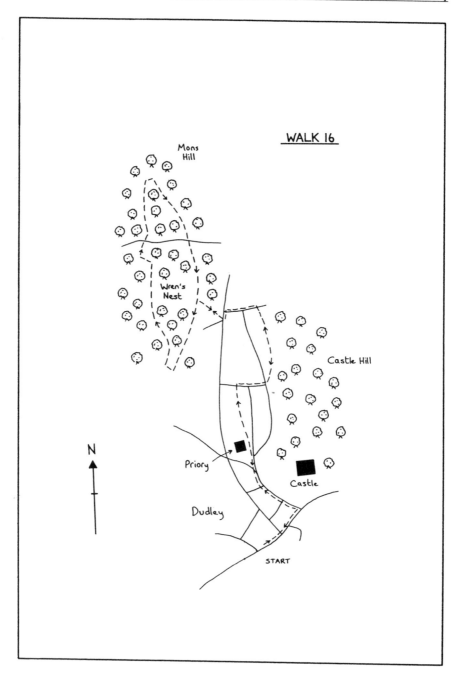

WALK 16

Priory ruins at Dudley

Domesday Book reveals that the Normans made it the centre of a huge manorial estate which included the then tiny and insignificant village of Birmingham. Dudley Castle, originally founded in the late 11th century by William Fitz Ansculf, one of the followers of William the Conqueror, was the stronghold of the medieval Lords of Dudley. The present buildings belong to two main periods: first the early 14th century when the imposing keep was erected, and secondly the 16th century when the castle was remodelled by John Dudley, Earl of Northumberland, in order to make it a more comfortable and palatial residence. The defences of the castle were destroyed after the Civil War. There is a Visitor Centre and audio-visual display and Dudley Zoo, founded in the 1930s, is within the castle grounds.

**B.** These sparse ruins are of the small Cluniac priory of St James, founded in the 12th century by Gervase Paganel, Lord of Dudley, and dissolved by Henry VIII in 1536. They mainly comprise the church, especially the west front, and the foundations of some of the domestic buildings grouped around the cloister.

**C.** At the Castle Mill Canal Basin, lying at the base of Castle Hill, are the entrances to the Dudley Tunnels, created to link the Earl of Dudley's coal mines with the Birmingham Canal and the main canal network.

**D.** The prominent and thickly-wooded limestone hill of Wren's Nest has been extensively quarried for centuries. Initially the stone was extracted mainly for building purposes – both the castle and priory at Dudley were built from it – but later it was used as an agricultural fertiliser and in the local iron industries.

Wren's Nest is now a much-visited National Nature Reserve, of great geological importance and renowned for its fossils, perfectly preserved in the limestone and dating back to over 400 million years ago when the area was covered by coral reefs and tropical seas. One particular fossil, regularly found by quarrymen in the 19th century, was nicknamed the 'Dudley Bug'. As a result of centuries of quarrying – which only ceased in the 1920s – the hill is honeycombed by caverns and underground workings. There are two observation platforms, both passed on the route. The first one enables you to see the Seven Sisters Caverns, which run 328 feet (100m) below the hill and are linked by canal to the Castle Mill Basin. From the second platform, you view the spectacular geological formations at the base of the quarry which reveal the ripple marks on the rocks made by the action of the sea that once covered them.

**E.** The adjoining Mons Hill – still part of the Wren's Nest Nature Reserve – was also extensively quarried in the past but is now clothed with mature ash woodland. From the summit there are fine views over the Black Country.

# 17. Tipton and Dudley Port

**Start/Parking:** Tipton, at corner of Owen Street and Albion Street, near station and on south side of canal – grid ref. 956925

**Distance:** 4 miles (6.4km)

**Category:** Easy

**Refreshments:** Pubs at Tipton, Barge and Barrel by Factory Bridge

**Terrain:** Whole of the route is along canal towpaths

**OS Maps:** Landranger 139, Explorer 219

**Public transport:** Buses from Wolverhampton and West Bromwich; trains from Wolverhampton and Birmingham

---

## Discover:

This is a walk in the heart of what was once the most heavily industrialised and built-up part of the Black Country and even less than 30 years ago, to suggest a walk between Tipton and Dudley Port would have been greeted with howls of sarcastic laughter and expressions of doubt about your mental state. However times change and this route, which utilises the towpaths of three canals – Birmingham New Main Line, Birmingham Old Main Line and Netherton Branch – is enjoyable, pleasant, highly interesting and, in places, surprisingly rural. It enables you to appreciate aspects of both the past history of the area and some of the recent changes.

## Route Directions:

Start by crossing the canal bridge towards Tipton station and immediately turn left and head down to the towpath of the New Main Line Canal. Follow it past Factory Locks to Factory Bridge, where the New and Old Main Line canals between Birmingham and Wolverhampton join (A). Turn sharp right, by the Barge and Barrel pub, to cross the footbridge just passed under and from the bridge, the Rowley Hills and Dudley Castle can be seen above the roof lines.

Continue beside the Old Main Line Canal. Over on the other side are the Old Malthouse Stables, one of the few remaining traditional canal buildings. The towpath leads back to Tipton – scarcely ¼ mile (0.4km) from the start – where you pass the Fountain Inn (B). Continue along the

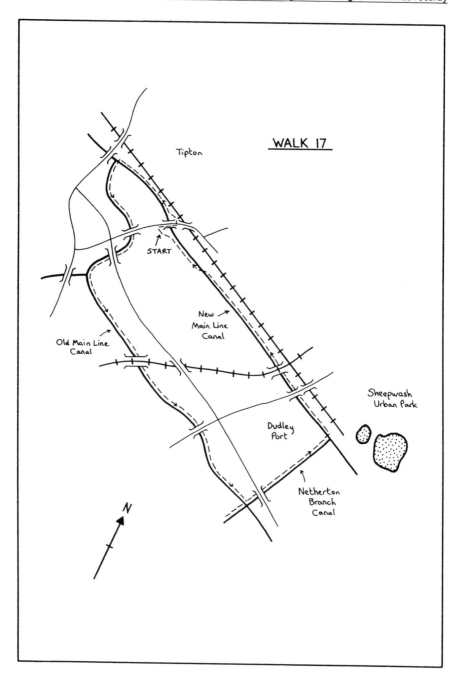

WALK 17

Tipton

START

New
Main Line
Canal

Old Main Line
Canal

Dudley
Port

Sheepwash
Urban Park

Netherton
Branch
Canal

N

The Old Main Line Canal near Tipton

towpath, passing another canal junction on the right where the Dudley Branch leads past the Black Country Museum, through the Dudley Tunnels beneath Castle Hill and on to join the Stourbridge Canal.

After passing under a railway bridge, the surroundings become more rural and you keep beside the canal as far as the aqueduct, which carries it over the Netherton Branch Canal. Turn left to descend steps to the Netherton Branch and turn sharp right along the towpath, passing beside some attractive old canalside cottages and under the aqueduct, to the entrance to the Netherton Tunnel (C). Retrace your steps to pass under the aqueduct again and keep along the towpath in a straight line to the junction with the New Main Line Canal at Dudley Port. As you turn right to first cross a footbridge over the Netherton Branch and then turn left to cross one over the main canal, there is a striking – if not exactly picturesque – view over a typical Black Country landscape. The view includes the lakes of the Sheepwash Urban Park, an excellent habitat for water birds.

After crossing the bridges, keep by the New Main Line Canal back to Tipton, passing Dudley Port station. On this final part of the walk – as on the opening stretch – the main railway line runs parallel to the canal, both of them in a straight line. At Watery Lane Junction – where there are currently plans to build a marina – turn sharp right to cross a metal bridge over the canal (it has the date 1880 on it) and continue along the other side. About 100 yards (91m) after passing under the bridge by Tipton station, turn left through a metal barrier to a road and turn sharp left back to the start.

## Features of Interest:

**A.** The Old Main Line Canal was first built in 1769 by Brindley to carry coal from the mines around Wednesbury to Birmingham. In 1772, it was extended to Wolverhampton. It was designed to follow the contours of the land and avoid any major engineering projects. Because of greatly increased traffic, Telford was commissioned to upgrade the canal in the 1820s and the result was the New Main Line Canal. Unlike Brindley's canal, this runs more or less in a straight line through cuttings and across embankments.

**B.** In the middle of the 19th century, the Fountain Inn was the home and training centre of the 'Tipton Slasher', a well-known champion boxer.

**C.** For details of the Netherton Tunnel see Walk 15.

# 18. Baggeridge Country Park, Himley Hall and Wombourne

**Start/Parking:** Baggeridge Country Park, off A463 at Gospel End Village – grid ref. 898931

**Distance:** 8 miles (12.9km)

**Category:** Moderate

**Refreshments:** Himley Park Café by Himley Hall, Ye Olde Station Tea Shoppe at the former Wombourne station, pubs at Wombourne

**Terrain:** Field and woodland paths, parkland, long stretch along a disused railway track and a short stretch of suburban walking

**OS Maps:** Landranger 139, Explorer 219

**Public transport:** Buses from Wolverhampton pass the entrance to Baggeridge Country Park

## Discover:

This attractive walk, just to the south west of Wolverhampton, divides into four distinct parts. First comes a pleasant stroll through the well-wooded terrain of Baggeridge Country Park and the adjoining Himley Park, passing the imposing 18th-century Himley Hall. This is followed by a 3 mile (4.8km) walk along a disused railway track. Then comes a short stretch of suburban walking through Wombourne and the final leg is across fields and through belts of woodland. The walking is easy and there are fine and extensive views over the surrounding Staffordshire countryside.

## Route Directions:

From the Visitor Centre, head downhill along a tarmac track – at a notice 'Start of Trails, Himley Hall and Pools' – and keep ahead along a path waymarked 'Baggeridge Circular Walk' (A). Continue along this winding path, following the regular Circular Walk signs, through woodland and across meadows. At one point, look out for a sign that directs you to turn sharp right and head downhill through a wooded valley, either above or beside a series of small pools on the right.

Following signs to Himley Hall, continue first beside the larger Spring Pool - here leaving the Baggeridge Circular Walk - then by a cascade and finally alongside the beautiful Island Pool. At the far end of the

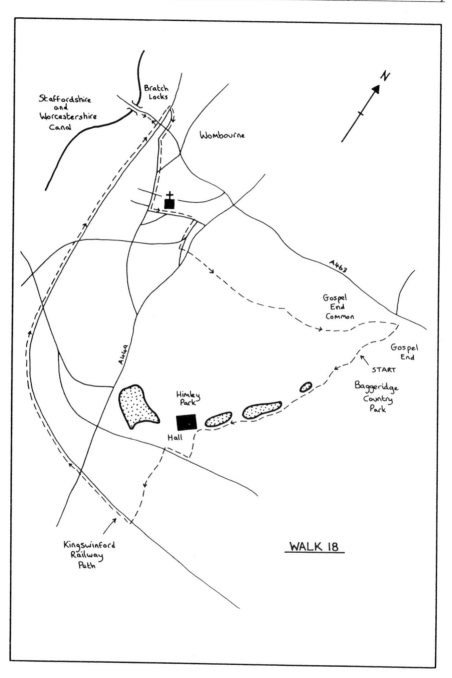

Staffordshire
and
Worcestershire
Canal

Bratch
Locks

Wombourne

A463

Gospel
End
Common

Gospel
End

START

Baggeridge
Country
Park

Himley
Park

Hall

Kingswinford
Railway
Path

WALK 18

pool, bear left through a kissing gate to leave Baggeridge Country Park and bear left along a tarmac track to continue through the adjacent Himley Park. Keep beside Rock Pool to Himley Hall (B), turn left along a drive at a T-junction and at a fork, take the left-hand drive to pass through gates onto a road. Turn right and at a public footpath sign, turn left along the track to Home Farm. Go through a gate, continue past the farm along an enclosed track, pass beside a gate and keep along the track to a disused railway bridge. Turn right in front of it onto an uphill track and bear right to join the Kingswinford Railway Path (C).

Keep along this disused railway track for just over 3 miles (4.8km) as far as the former Wombourne station building, now a tea room. The track, tree-lined all the way, sometimes runs across the top of embankments and sometimes plunges through deep cuttings and after passing the car park and picnic area at Himley, goes through the middle of Himley Plantation. Just before reaching Wombourne station, turn right to a tarmac drive and turn right again to a road. Turn right along it for a short detour to see the Bratch Locks on the Staffordshire and Worcestershire Canal (D). Retrace your steps and opposite the drive to the Station car park, turn right along Station Road. Now follows a short stretch of suburban walking through Wombourne.

Keep ahead at traffic lights, turn left at a T-junction along Church Road, passing the mainly 19th-century church, and continue to the A449. Just before reaching it, turn right along Battlefield Hill and opposite a lane on the right, turn left along the edge of a triangular green and carefully cross the busy A449 – there is a stile on the central reservation of the dual carriageway. On the other side go through a kissing gate, at a public footpath sign, and walk along a hedge-lined path to a gate. After going through, bear left to continue along a left field edge and in the field corner, keep ahead into woodland to a stile. Climb it, continue through the trees, bearing right by a ruined brick building, and after the path emerges from the wood, it heads across a field to enter another belt of woodland. Head uphill through it and then the route continues along a track. Just before reaching a farm, bear right off the track to climb a stile and at the junction of paths and tracks ahead, keep straight ahead to re-enter woodland.

Continue across the open heathland of Gospel End Common (E), bearing right to a T-junction. Turn left to another one and turn right onto a tarmac drive. Follow this drive through the woodlands of the country park, heading gently downhill to return to the start.

## Features of Interest:

**A.** The area covered by Baggeridge Country Park, like the adjoining Himley Park, belonged to the Earls of Dudley and the southern part – where the pools are – was part of the landscaped parkland surrounding Himley Hall. From the late 19th century onwards, the north of the park was mined for coal but after the closure of the colliery in 1968, it was acquired by the local council who landscaped it and opened it as a country park in 1983. The park is a varied and attractive mixture of woodland, heathland, meadows, streams and pools. Most of the meadows have been reseeded above the colliery waste and the former spoil tips are now grassy hills. One of these has a toposcope.

**B.** The dignified Georgian mansion of Himley Hall, built around 1740, was the family home of the Earls of Dudley and is situated amidst sweeping parkland landscaped by 'Capability' Brown. Proximity to the noise and squalor of industry caused the family to desert it for Witley Court in the Worcestershire countryside but they returned after the First World War and in the 1930s, the hall was frequently visited by the Prince of Wales, later Edward VIII. It was later acquired by the National Coal Board but now belongs to Dudley Council and is open to the public during the spring and summer.

Himley Hall

**C.** The railway line was originally owned by the Great Western Railway and was built to serve the rural area to the west of the Black Country. It was never a great success; passenger services ceased in the 1930s and the line was finally closed in 1965. It was later converted into the present Kingswinsford Railway Path, a cycleway and footpath that runs for 5½ miles (8.9km).

**D.** The Staffordshire and Worcestershire Canal, designed by James Brindley and opened in 1772, was built to provide a link between the Trent and Mersey Canal at Great Haywood and the River Severn at Stourport. The three adjacent Bratch Locks and the octagonal toll house make a particularly interesting and attractive scene. Nearby is the Bratch Pumping Station, a superb and highly ornate example of Victorian architecture, opened in 1897, the year of the Diamond Jubilee, to supply water to the Wombourne and Bilston areas. It housed two steam engines, which remained in operation until 1960 when they were replaced by electric power.

**E.** Although only a remnant, Gospel End Common is invaluable as one of the few remaining areas of ancient heathland in the West Midlands. It forms part of Baggeridge Country Park.

# 19. Lichfield

**Start:** Market Square – grid ref. 117096

**Distance:** 2½ miles (4km)

**Category:** Easy

**Parking:** Lichfield

**Refreshments:** Plenty of pubs, restaurants and tea and coffee shops in Lichfield

**Terrain:** Easy town walking, plus parkland and a circuit of a pool

**Maps:** Pick up a street map at the Tourist Information Centre in Bore Street

**Public transport:** Lichfield is served by buses and trains from all the surrounding towns

## Discover:

Lichfield, seat of a bishop since the 7th century, is in many ways the archetypal English cathedral city. A number of attractive and mostly pedestrianised streets lead off from the Market Square and the cathedral stands in a dignified and secluded close on the edge of the small city. Apart from the glorious three-spired cathedral, Lichfield's main claim to fame is that Dr Johnson was born here. The route starts by Johnson's birthplace and statue, visits the major sites of historic interest and includes both a short walk through Beacon Park to the west of the cathedral and a circuit of Stowe Pool to the east.

## Route Directions:

Start in front of St Mary's church (A) by the Dr Johnson statue and turn down Breadmarket Street to the Guildhall (B). Turn right along Bore Street – there are some good Georgian houses on the left – and turn left along St John Street to St John's Hospital and Chapel (C). Retrace your steps along St John Street and keep ahead along Bird Street to Minster Pool. From here there is a particularly memorable view of the cathedral, with its three spires rising above the pool.

Opposite the Garden of Remembrance, turn left into Beacon Park and, at a path junction, turn right, in the Cathedral direction. Follow the path around a left bend, turn right at a T-junction and at the fork just ahead, bear right to cross Leomansley Brook and turn left alongside it.

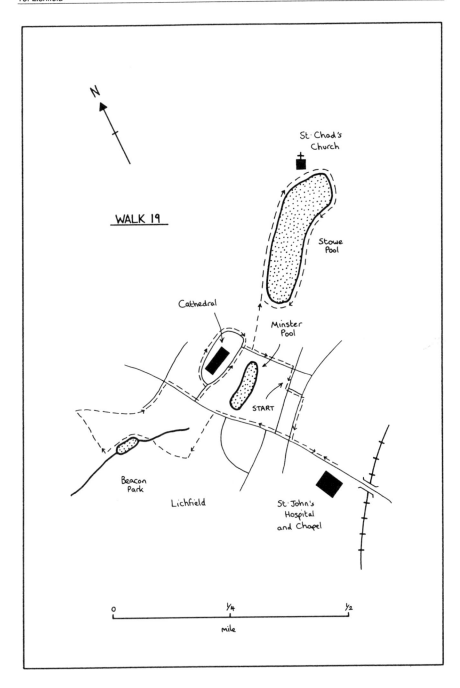

N

WALK 19

St. Chad's
Church

Stowe
Pool

Cathedral

Minster
Pool

START

Beacon
Park

Lichfield

St. John's
Hospital
and Chapel

0      ¼      ½
mile

The brook soon broadens into a small pool. The path bends right, passing a children's play area, to leave the park and at a Heart of England Way sign, turn right onto an enclosed path. This becomes a grassy path along the edge of the park and the route then continues along an enclosed tarmac track to emerge into a small car park.

Turn left along a lane to a crossroads, turn right, passing the Erasmus Darwin Centre (D), and turn left into the Close to walk up to the west front of the cathedral (E). At the far end of the Close, turn right along Dam Street and take the first turning on the left. Keep along a hedge-lined tarmac path, which continues along the edge of Stowe Pool, curving right at the far end to St Chad's church (F). Complete the circuit of the pool to return to Dam Street and turn left. The street, lined with more handsome Georgian houses and some older buildings, leads back into the Market Square.

## Features of Interest:

A. The Market Square, the focal point of Lichfield, is dominated by the large 19th-century St Mary's church, now a Heritage Centre displaying the city's history. In the centre of the square is a statue to Dr Johnson, Lichfield's most famous son, and nearby is his birthplace. He was born here in 1709 and the house is now a Johnson museum.

B. The Guildhall has a Victorian Gothic facade. Next to it is Donegal House, a handsome 18th-century town house, which now contains the tourist information centre and an exhibition devoted to the history of the area.

C. St John's Hospital and Chapel is regarded as one of the finest medieval brick buildings in the country. It was founded in 1135 by Augustinian canons as a place to accommodate pilgrims visiting the shrine of St Chad in the cathedral. In 1485 it was refounded as a residence for homeless men and is still inhabited today. The fine 15th-century chapel can be visited.

D. This was the home of Erasmus Darwin, grandfather of Charles Darwin and a noted scientist, inventor, philosopher and poet. It is now a museum to his life and work.

E. As well as being one of England's most beautiful medieval cathedrals, Lichfield has the distinction of being the only three-spired one. The diocese was founded around 669 by St Chad. The present cathedral was started around the end of the 12th century and com-

The three spires of Lichfield cathedral

pleted in the early 14th century. During the Civil War it suffered much destruction. It was besieged for three days, during which the central spire fell down, and at times was used as both a barracks and a stables. A thorough restoration was needed during the reign of Charles II, when the central tower and spire were rebuilt, and further substantial restorations took place in the 18th and 19th centuries. Chief glories of the cathedral are the unique three spires and the ornate west front. Although most of the statues on the latter are the work of the Victorians, it is one of the finest sights in England. The interior dates mainly from the 13th-century, apart from the early 14th-century Lady Chapel, the last part of the cathedral to be completed. The chapel contains 16th-century glass brought here from a Belgian monastery. The surroundings of the cathedral are delightful. It occupies a slightly elevated site on the edge of the small city and around it is a quiet close of dignified 17th- and 18th-century houses. The views of it are highly photogenic from all directions.

**F.** The church is medieval but the site is an ancient one for a Saxon church was founded here by St Chad, the first bishop of Lichfield, in the 7th century. Restorations took place in the 17th century, following damage in the Civil War, and again in the Victorian period.

# 20. Coventry

**Start:** Broadgate – grid ref. 334790

**Distance:** 2½ miles (4km)

**Category:** Easy

**Parking:** Coventry

**Refreshments:** Plenty of pubs, cafés and restaurants in Coventry

**Terrain:** Easy town walking

**Maps:** Pick up a street map from the Tourist Information Centre in Bayley Lane

**Public transport:** Coventry is served by buses and trains from all the surrounding towns and has coach and rail links with all parts of the country

## Discover:

To most people Coventry probably means three things: the story of Lady Godiva, wartime destruction, and its new cathedral. The city centre of Coventry was comprehensively destroyed by World War II bombing but individual buildings and streets remain – including short stretches of the medieval wall – to give some idea of what the pre-war city looked like. In the Middle Ages, Coventry was the fourth largest city in England and its prosperity was based on the wool trade. Economic stagnation followed the decline of the cloth industry in the 16$^{th}$ century but the city experienced a revival in the 19$^{th}$ century with the growth of ribbon weaving and watch making, and later the cycle and car industries. It also became a centre for armaments in the war, hence the bombing. After the war, Coventry became a symbol and pioneer of post-war planning as well as the home of a modern cathedral. The walk links together the remnants of Coventry's past with the city's post-war developments.

## Route Directions:

Start by the Lady Godiva statue (A) and, with your back to the Cathedral Lanes Shopping Centre, cross the road for a look at The Precinct (B). Return to the statue, pass to the right of it and turn right down Greyfriars Lane. On the left you pass Ford's Hospital (C) and a little further on is the tower and spire of Greyfriars church (D). Cross the road beyond the church, keep ahead along Warwick Road and turn right into Greyfriars

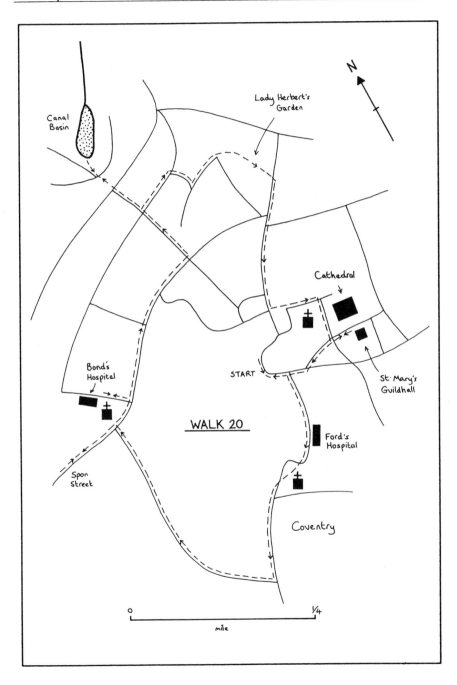

N

Canal
Basin

Lady Herbert's
Garden

Cathedral

Bond's
Hospital

START

St. Mary's
Guildhall

WALK 20

Ford's
Hospital

Spon
Street

Coventry

0                                        ¼

mile

Road. The road curves right up to St John's church (E). In front of the church, turn left to walk along Spon Street (F). Return to the church and turn left into Hill Street to see Bond's Hospital (G).

Retrace your steps and turn left along Corporation Street. A brief detour to the left along Upper Well Street enables you to see a section of Coventry's medieval town wall on the right. Continue along Corporation Street as far as Bishop Street, turn left and head uphill to cross a footbridge over the ring road and enter the Canal Basin (H).Retrace your steps over the footbridge and back down Bishop Street and turn left into Tower Street. Take the first turning on the right, turn left in front of the Museum of British Road Transport into Cook Street and where it ends, pass under Cook Street Gate. Turn right to walk through Lady Herbert's Garden, following another section of the medieval wall, and turn right along a road, passing the Swanswell Gate (J).

At a crossroads, keep ahead along Trinity Street and turn left up steps into Priory Row to continue between the foundations of the medieval priory on the left and Holy Trinity church (K) on the right. Take the first turning on the right and turn left along Bayley Lane. The cathedral is on the left (L) and St Mary's Guildhall (M) on the right.

Retrace your steps along Bayley Lane and keep ahead along Pepper Lane, which bears left to High Street. Turn right back to Broadgate.

## Features of Interest:

**A.** The legend of Lady Godiva is well-known. She allegedly rode naked through the streets of Coventry in order to persuade her husband, Leofric Earl of Mercia, not to increase the tax burden on the citizens. Apart from Peeping Tom, no one looked and apparently the protest was successful.

**B.** The Precinct was the pioneer for post-war redevelopment of town centres in Britain and therefore has some historic significance. Now it looks quite commonplace but at the time – the early 1950s – it was revolutionary in its concepts of separating people from traffic and having shopping on two levels.

**C.** These almshouses, endowed in 1509 under the will of William Ford, are among the finest examples of timber-framed buildings in England.

**D.** The spire of Greyfriars church is one of the three spires for which Coventry has always been famous – the other two are the cathedral and Holy Trinity church. The church originally belonged to a Franciscan friary, which was demolished when the friaries were suppressed by Henry VIII in 1542. Its successor, built in 1832, was destroyed by fire in World War II.

E. The church was originally built in 1344 to serve the Guild of St John the Baptist, alternatively known as Bablake College. After the guilds were dissolved in 1548, the church fell into disuse and during the Cromwellian era it was used as a prison. The hostile reception that the prisoners received from the local citizens is claimed to be the origin of the phrase 'to be sent to Coventry'. The church was later refounded as a parish church in 1734 and restored in the 19$^{th}$ century.

F. Most of the attractive medieval buildings in Spon Street have been brought from other parts of the city and re-erected here.

G. Bond's Hospital occupies the site of the medieval College of Bablake. The almshouses were founded in 1506 under the will of Thomas Bond and later became a boys' school. The buildings were enlarged and restored in the 19$^{th}$ century.

H. The Coventry Canal was built in 1769 to provide a link between Coventry and the Trent and Mersey Canal at Fradley near Lichfield and the Y-shaped basin was constructed at the same time. There are some impressive 19$^{th}$-century restored warehouses.

J. Not many people know that short lengths of Coventry's medieval wall still remain and the finest stretch runs through Lady Herbert's Garden, laid out between 1930 and 1939 as a memorial to the wife of Sir Alfred Herbert, a local industrialist and philanthropist. Cook Street and Swanswell are the only surviving gates; both probably date from the 15$^{th}$ century.

K. The imposing Holy Trinity church was founded in the 12$^{th}$ century. The spire had to be replaced in the 17$^{th}$ century following destruction by a great storm in 1666. Opposite are the foundations of the Benedictine priory, originally founded by Leofric and Godiva in 1043. This was a huge church and during the Middle Ages served as a second cathedral for the Lichfield diocese. It was destroyed following Henry VIII's dissolution of the monasteries in the 1530s.

L. The cathedral that was gutted during the terrible bombing raids on the night of 14 November 1940 was a grand 15$^{th}$-century parish

The bombed ruins of the old Coventry Cathedral

church, one of the largest in the country, which had only been raised to cathedral status with the founding of the diocese of Coventry in 1918. Apart from the outside walls, only the tower and superb spire survived; the latter is the third tallest in the country, only exceeded by the cathedrals of Salisbury and Norwich. When the new Coventry Cathedral was built, it was decided to retain the ruins of the old and to align the new one at right angles to them, an imaginative concept. A glass wall at the north end allows the old to be seen from the new and vice versa. The new cathedral was built from local pink sandstone to the design of Basil Spence and was completed in 1962. Among its most outstanding features are Epstein's sculpture of St Michael the Archangel on the outside and Graham Sutherland's huge tapestry of Christ that dominates the views of the interior.

**M.** St Mary's Hall, a superb example of a medieval guildhall, was originally built in 1340-42 for the merchant guild of St Mary. It was later enlarged and altered at the end of the 15th century. The great hall has a magnificent 14th-century timber roof and below is a vaulted undercroft.

# 21. Ironbridge Gorge

**Start:** Ironbridge, on the north (town) side of the bridge – grid ref. 673035

**Distance:** 6 miles (9.7km)

**Category:** Fairly strenuous

**Parking:** The Iron Bridge car park, on south side of bridge

**Refreshments:** Pubs and cafés at Ironbridge

**Terrain:** Fairly hilly walk along woodland and field paths, with a final stretch through the Severn Gorge

**OS Maps:** Landranger 127, Explorer 242

**Public transport:** Buses from Telford town centre and Shrewsbury

## Discover:

This fascinating walk takes you through part of the Ironbridge Gorge and the adjacent Coalbrookdale, the alleged birthplace of the Industrial Revolution and one of Britain's World Heritage Sites. Although not a long walk, you really need to devote almost the whole day to it if you want to combine it with visiting the various places of interest. As well as passing by some of the renowned industrial monuments, there is also the chance to visit the ruins of a medieval abbey. The unique historical importance of this area is enhanced by the grand views of the Wrekin and across the Severn valley and the walk concludes with a stroll by the river through the gorge.

## Route Directions:

Begin at the Iron Bridge (A) and, facing the church, pass to the right of the Tontine Hotel and climb a flight of steps which leads up to the church, going under a tunnel. At the top, turn left along a road, passing to the right of the church, continue uphill, by attractive brick cottages, follow the road as it curves right and at a junction, look out for where a Shropshire Way sign directs you to turn sharply left onto a track.

At a public footpath sign, turn right along a path through woodland, turn right again at a T-junction and at the fork immediately ahead, take the left-hand lower path. At the next fork take the left-hand lower path again, signposted to Paradise, and the path descends steeply through the trees. Keep ahead at a crossroads, descend steps and continue to a tarmac track. Turn left down a tarmac track to a T-junction, turn right along a lane to a road and then continue along it through Coalbrookdale.

After passing the Rayburn Coalbrookdale Foundry (on the site where Abraham Darby first smelted iron with coke in 1709), bear left along a road which leads down to the Museum of Iron (B). Keep to the left of it and the road bends right and passes under a disused railway viaduct to a T-junction. Turn right alongside the arches of the viaduct and at the next T-junction, turn left uphill, passing the Darby Houses and a sign to the Quaker Burial Ground on the left.

At a public footpath sign to Ropewalk, bear right through a gate and walk along an enclosed, wooded track. The track later keeps along the left edge of Ropewalk Meadow and then continues through the fine woodland of Loamhole Dingle. After passing through a fence gap, the well-waymarked path bends left, heads steeply uphill – via steps in places – and continues winding through the trees to eventually reach a stile on the edge of the woodland. Climb it, walk across a field, keeping to the left of a house, and go through a gate onto a tarmac drive. Turn left and the drive bends left to emerge onto a lane. Turn right, crossing a bridge over the busy A4169 and, at a Shropshire Way sign, turn left along a track.

Pass to the right of a house and in front of gates to a farm, turn right over a stile and walk diagonally across a field. Bear right to continue along its left edge, climb a stile and as you continue across the next field – making for its left edge – there are fine views ahead of the Wrekin and to the left over the Severn valley. Look out for where a Shropshire Way sign directs you to turn left steeply downhill through a hedge gap. Bear right along the top right edge of a sloping field and continue into woodland to a stile. After climbing it, turn left along a steadily descending tree-lined track – it later narrows to a path – to a tarmac drive and bear left down to a road. Turn left and take the first turning on the right, signposted to Much Wenlock, Ironbridge and Broseley. For the brief detour to Buildwas Abbey (C), keep ahead to cross the bridge over the River Severn but the route continues to the left along the road signposted to Ironbridge.

After about 200 yards (183m), look out for a stile and a Severn Way sign on the right. Here there is a choice of either taking the riverside path – which is narrow and can be overgrown and quite difficult in places – or, if you wish to avoid these potential problems, continuing

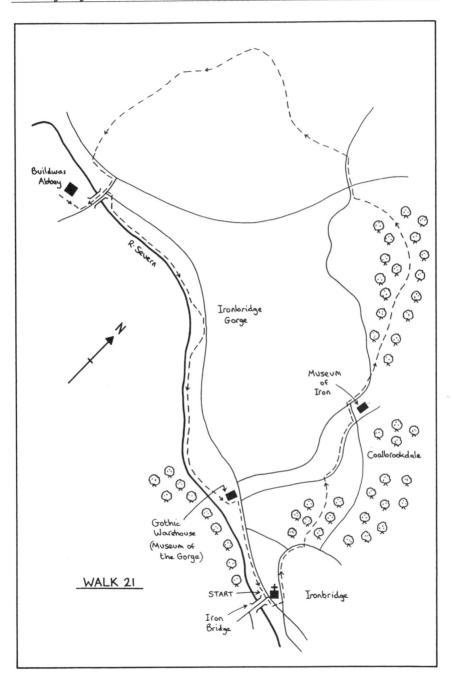

WALK 21

along the road as far as the next Severn Way sign, about 3/4 mile (1.2km) further on.

For the riverside path, turn right over the stile, walk across a meadow and continue along the riverbank. Climb a stile, continue through trees – there are steps in places – and pass under a disused railway bridge. This is the awkward stretch where the path is likely to be overgrown and it is narrow and uneven at times. Continue winding through trees between road and river and when you see a stile, turn left up steps and climb it onto the road. Turn right and after 50 yards (46m) – at a Severn Way sign just after the 'Welcome to Ironbridge' notice – turn right through a hedge gap and descend steps.

This is where those walkers who have stayed on the road to avoid the difficult riverside path leave it. Turn left to follow the path through an area of scrub – there are again some narrow and potentially overgrown stretches – going under two bridges and passing in front of the four pink cooling towers of the power station on the opposite bank. After the second bridge (Albert Edward Bridge), you soon reach the Ironbridge Rowing Club building and from here conditions become easier as you continue through Dale End Riverside Park along the right edge of a meadow beside the Severn.

Continue along a wide tarmac track through the gorge, pass beside a gate and keep along the riverside path as far as the Gothic Warehouse (D). Turn left up steps to the road. turn right and follow the road back to the Iron Bridge.

## Features of Interest:

**A.** The Iron Bridge, the first of its kind in the world, is the focal point of a series of early industrial monuments in and around the Ironbridge Gorge. The combination of plenty of timber from the nearby woods plus local supplies of coal, iron and limestone made this part of Shropshire an early centre of the iron industry. The event that transformed the industry and made the area one of the cradles of the Industrial Revolution was Abraham Darby's first successful smelting of iron ore with coke instead of charcoal at his Coalbrookdale works in 1709. This freed the iron industry from its dependence on timber – which was becoming scarce – and enabled it to expand and use coal, which was plentiful. A new bridge over the Severn was needed because Darby's invention increased the commercial importance of the area. It was decided to use iron and appropriately this came from Coalbrookdale, cast by Abraham Darby III. When the

The Iron Bridge, spanning the River Severn

bridge was opened in 1779, it was regarded as the wonder of the age and attracted immense interest and enthusiasm. There is an exhibition and information centre in the Tollhouse at the south end of the bridge. The town of Ironbridge developed on its north side.

**B.** The Museum of Iron is housed in a warehouse which is adjacent to the original furnace where the first Abraham Darby successfully smelted iron with coke in 1709. Nearby are the Darby Houses – Rosehill House and Dale House – former homes of the family of ironmasters.

**C.** The peaceful and mellowed ruins of Buildwas Abbey, founded in 1135 on the banks of the Severn, are a complete contrast to the industrial monuments of the Ironbridge Gorge. It was a small monastery and had a fairly uneventful history until its closure by Henry VIII in 1536. There are substantial remains of the 12th-century church and a fine vaulted chapter house.

**D.** This former warehouse of the Coalbrookdale Company now houses the Museum of the Gorge, an exhibition which tells the whole story of the Ironbridge Gorge.

# 22. Tong and Boscobel House

**Start:** Tong, by the church – grid ref. 795074

**Distance:** 7½ miles (12.1km)

**Category:** Moderate

**Parking:** Roadside parking by Tong church

**Refreshments:** Tearoom at Boscobel House

**Terrain:** Tracks and field paths across flat country, with a short stretch along a quiet and narrow lane

**OS Maps:** Landranger 127, Explorer 242

**Public transport:** Buses from Wellington, Telford town centre and Wolverhampton

## Discover:

From the imposing medieval church at Tong, the walk heads across fields and past farms to the meagre but attractively-sited ruins of White Ladies Priory. About 1 mile (1.6km) further on along a lane is Boscobel House which, along with a neighbouring oak tree, played a crucial role in the escape of Charles II into exile following Cromwell's victory in the Civil War and the execution of his father. Much of the return leg is along an attractive, enclosed track. From several points on the route, there are fine views looking across the flat landscape to the Wrekin and some of the other Shropshire hills.

## Route Directions:

Facing the church (A), turn left along the road and where it bends right to the main road, bear left along a concrete track which runs parallel to the M54 (beyond the hedge on the right). The track later becomes a rough one and where it bears left towards a farm, keep ahead through a gate and walk along a path – still parallel to the motorway – to another gate.

After going through that one, turn left along a concrete track, keep to the right of farm buildings and at a Monarch's Way sign, turn right onto another track. Go through a gate, turn left and continue along the track, by a hedge on the left. Go through another gate, keep ahead to the field corner, follow the path to the right and turn left through a gate. Con-

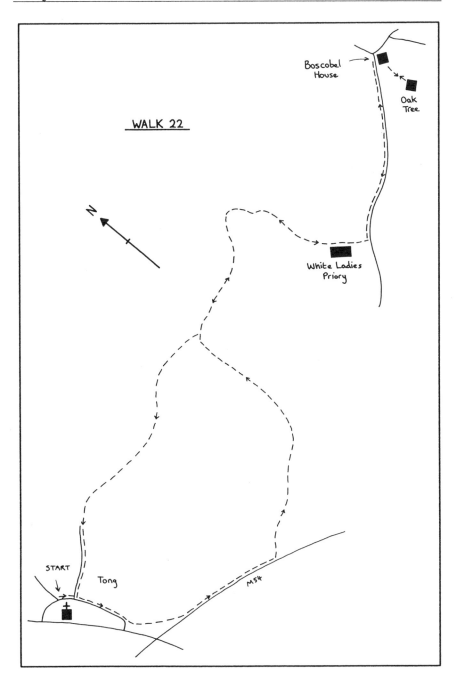

WALK 22

N

Boscobel
House

Oak
Tree

White Ladies
Priory

START

Tong

M54

tinue through a belt of trees, walk along the right edge of a field, keep ahead along the left edge of the next field and go through a gate to a T-junction. Note that the return to Tong is to the left here but in order to visit White Ladies Priory and Boscobel House, turn right along a hedge-lined track to a tarmac drive. Keep ahead and the drive bends right to a farm. Turn left through a gate in front of the farmhouse, bear right across a stable yard, turn right through a gate in the corner, turn left through another gate and keep ahead along an enclosed path. Go through a gate, walk along the left field edge, go through another gate in the corner and continue along a tree-lined path, passing to the left of the ruins of White Ladies Priory (B). Continue past the priory to a lane, turn left and follow this winding lane gently uphill to the entrance to Boscobel House (C).

Retrace your steps to where you joined the enclosed, hedge-lined track at a T-junction and continue along it. It is called Hubbal Lane. After passing a farm on the right, the track becomes a narrow lane which leads back to Tong church.

## Features of Interest:

**A.** It is rare to find such a large and impressive cruciform church in what is no more than a hamlet. In 1868 Elihu Burritt called it 'this miniature cathedral' and a 'Village Westminster Abbey'. The reason for its size and grandeur is that it was a collegiate church, founded in the early 15th century by Lady Isabel, wife the lord of the manor who resided at the now vanished Tong Castle. It is a superb example of the Perpendicular style and the imposing central tower is partly octagonal. Inside is a large collection of tombs and monuments to the Vernon and Stanley families, owners of Tong Castle, and the fan vaulting in the early 16th-century Golden Chapel is usually only seen in cathedrals or some of the grander college chapels at Oxford and Cambridge.

**B.** The ruins are those of a small, 12th-century Augustinian nunnery and comprise little more than the priory church. Of the later house that was built on the site – which like Boscobel sheltered Charles II – nothing remains.

**C.** The chief claim to fame of this modest and picturesque, early 17th-century timber-framed house is the role it played in hiding Charles II from Cromwell's troops in the days that followed his final defeat at the battle of Worcester in September 1651. The king came

Boscobel House and the Royal Oak

to Boscobel because its owners, the Giffard family, were Catholics and loyal to the Crown, as were several other families in the locality. For part of the time he hid in the house and for one whole day, when the place was teeming with Cromwell's soldiers, he was forced to perch – rather uncomfortably – in the branches of a nearby oak tree. The present tree is probably a descendant of the one in which Charles hid. The original was largely destroyed in later years by over-zealous souvenir hunters. After he left Boscobel House, the king made his way to the south coast and then across the Channel to the continent where he remained in exile for the next nine years, until the monarchy was restored in 1660. As the home of a Catholic family, Boscobel has the usual priest holes and hiding places and an added attraction is the garden, laid out in the formal 17th-century style.

# 23. Brewood and Chillington Hall

**Start:** Brewood, The Square – grid ref. 884088

**Distance:** 5 miles (8km)

**Category:** Easy

**Parking:** Brewood

**Refreshments:** Pubs and Connoisseur Restaurant and Tearoom at Brewood

**Terrain:** A combination of meadows, parkland, quiet lanes and pleasant walking along a canal towpath

**OS Maps:** Landranger 127, Explorer 242

**Public transport:** Buses from Wolverhampton and Penkridge

## Discover:

Near both the start and end of the walk there is some very attractive walking beside the Shropshire Union Canal. The remainder of the route is through woodland and across fields and parkland, passing the entrance to the 18<sup>th</sup>-century Chillington Hall. Brewood is an exceptionally attractive and interesting village with an imposing church and there are fine views of it across the fields from the canal towpath.

## Route Directions:

Begin by walking along the road signposted to St Mary and St Chad Church (A), pass to the right of the church and turn left at a T-junction. Almost immediately turn right, at public footpath and Staffordshire Way signs, go under an arch between cottages and walk along an enclosed path. The path bends first right and then left and continues to a T-junction.

Turn left, almost immediately turn right over a stile and walk along the left edge of two fields, climbing a stile. After climbing a second stile, head across the next field and in the corner, climb another stile onto the towpath of the Shropshire Union Canal (B). Turn left, passing under Dean's Hall Bridge, and walk along the towpath as far as the third bridge – Avenue Bridge (no 10) (C). After passing under it, turn left up steps and at the top, turn left again to cross it.

At the three-way fork immediately ahead, take the middle path

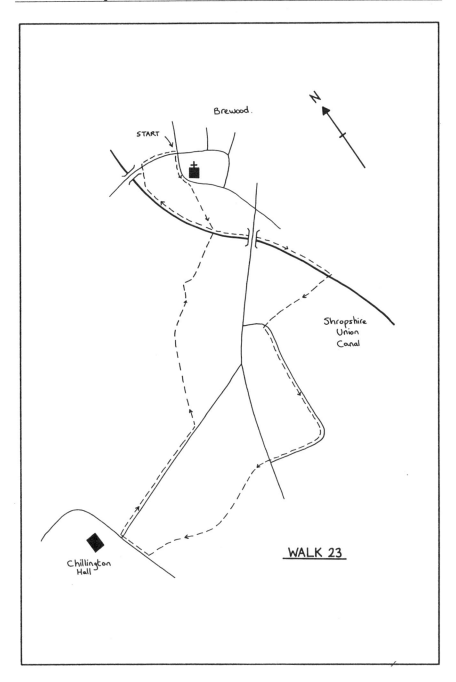

Brewood.

START

N

Shropshire
Union
Canal

Chillington
Hall

WALK 23

through trees – this is the Lower Avenue – to emerge onto a lane by a small parking area. Turn left along the narrow lane, follow it around a right bend to a T-junction and take the track ahead. This track becomes tree- and hedge-lined, curves left and narrows to a path. Later the route continues along a well-surfaced track to a narrow lane. Turn right along it to the entrance to Chillington Hall from where you get a fine view of the facade of the hall (D). Just before reaching it, turn right along another straight, narrow lane which runs parallel to the Upper Avenue and, after ½ mile (0.8km), turn left, at a public footpath sign, to climb a stile, here rejoining the Staffordshire Way.

Bear right, following waymarked posts, cross the Avenue and continue to a stile. Climb it, walk along an enclosed path, go through a kissing gate and continue by the right field edge to go through another kissing gate in the far corner. Turn right along a winding, hedge-lined track to a T-junction and turn right again to follow a tree-lined track to Dean's Hall Bridge. Turn left over a stile to descend steps to the canal towpath and walk along it to the second bridge (no 14). In front of the bridge, climb steps onto the road opposite the Bridge Inn and turn right to return to The Square.

## Features of Interest:

**A.** Brewood is an exceptionally attractive village with a number of 17th- and 18th-century buildings – and some older ones – around The Square and along the nearby side streets. The most striking of these is 'Speedwell Castle', a Gothic folly built around the middle of the 18th century by a local eccentric, reputedly from his horse racing winnings. In the Middle Ages Brewood lay within the boundaries of a royal forest and the manor belonged to the Bishops of Lichfield. This may partly explain why it has such an unusually large and fine church. Although heavily restored by the Victorians, the church of St Mary and St Chad was mostly built in the 13th century. The 15th-century tower and spire, a prominent landmark, rises to 169 feet (51m). Inside are tombs of the Giffard family, who lived at nearby Chillington Hall.

**B.** The Shropshire Union Canal is one of Telford's great engineering achievements and was completed in 1834. It joins the Staffordshire and Worcestershire Canal just north of Wolverhampton and links the Birmingham and Black Country canal system with Shropshire, Cheshire, North Wales and the Mersey.

Avenue Bridge on the Shropshire Union Canal

**C.** Avenue Bridge is a good example of the power of the 19th-century aristocracy. Telford designed it in an elegant Classical style in order that it would harmonise with Chillington Hall and the parkland setting and thus be acceptable to the Giffards. The canal itself runs through a deep cutting here so that it could not be seen from the house.

**D.** The Giffard family have held the Chillington estate since the 12th century. The same family also owned Boscobel House (see Walk 22). Chillington Hall, a handsome Georgian building, was built in 1724 and enlarged in the 1780s. Capability Brown landscaped the park and the Lower and Upper Avenues were designed as impressive driveways to the hall.

# 24. Doxey Marshes and Stafford Castle

**Start:** Stafford, Market Square – grid ref. 923234

**Distance:** 5½ miles (8.9km)

**Category:** Easy

**Parking:** Stafford

**Refreshments:** Pubs and cafés in Stafford

**Terrain:** Riverside and field paths, plus disused railway tracks that have been converted into footpaths and cycle ways

**OS Maps:** Landranger 127, Explorer 6 (to be renumbered 244)

**Public transport:** Stafford is served by buses and trains from all the surrounding towns

## Discover:

From the centre of Stafford you initially follow riverside paths to Doxey Marshes, a local nature reserve. The route heads back along a disused railway track to the edge of the town and then continues gently uphill to the remains of Stafford Castle. After descending, another stretch of former railway track leads back to the River Sow and the town centre.

## Route Directions:

The walk begins in the Market Square (A) and with your back to the Shire Hall, turn left along Greengate Street to the Ancient High House. Turn right beside it along St Mary's Passage, passing to the left of St Mary's church, and turn left down picturesque Church Lane. Cross a road, continue down Water Street to a T-junction and keep ahead into Victoria Park.

Follow a tarmac path through the park, turn left to cross a footbridge over the River Sow and turn right alongside the river to a road. Cross over, keep ahead along South Street and continue along a tarmac riverside path, following the river around a right bend to cross another road. Continue beside the river, passing under two bridges, as far as a track – this is part of the disused Stafford to Uttoxeter railway – and turn right along it, crossing the river, for a brief incursion into Doxey Marshes

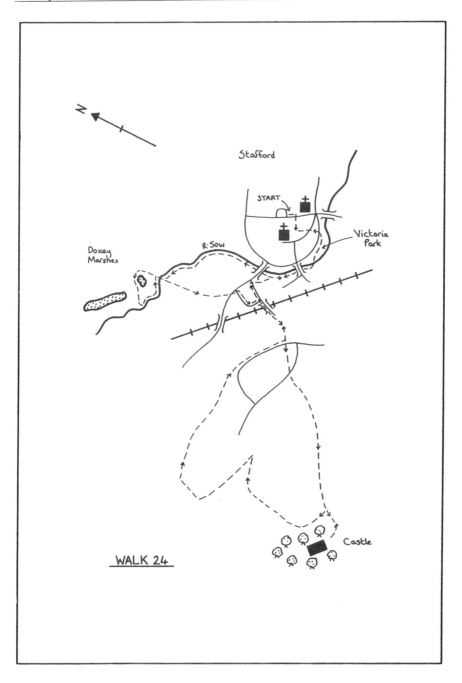

Stafford

START

Victoria Park

R. Sow

Doxey Marshes

WALK 24

Castle

Nature Reserve (B). On approaching a cemetery, turn left through a fence gap – at post no 12 – and bear left across grass, making for the field corner where you turn left over a stile. Keep ahead, passing post no 11 and a stone pyramid (this indicates the gift of Doxey Marshes to the Staffordshire Nature Conservation Trust in 1983), and at post no 10, turn right onto a path which heads across to the river. Turn sharp left and follow the meandering Sow back to the disused railway track.

Turn right and walk along the track to where it bends left on approaching a road. Continue as far as a stile on the right, climb it, turn left along the road and turn right into Jermingham Street, signposted as a cycle route to Derrington. Turn left at the end of the street and at a T-junction, turn right and cross a railway bridge. Where the road ends, keep ahead along a tarmac track, go through a kissing gate, cross a road and continue along the right edge of a green. Cross another road and turn right, at a public bridleway sign, along a path which bears slightly left to a footpath post.

Keep by a hedge on the left and later continue along an attractive, hedge- and tree-lined path which heads across a golf course, giving fine views of Stafford Castle. After climbing a stile, keep ahead across grass and, if visiting the castle (C), climb another stile; otherwise turn right and walk diagonally across a field towards the wooded castle mound. Climb a stile in the far corner, turn right – in the Doxey direction – and head downhill along the right edge of two fields. In the corner of the second field, turn right through a gate and continue diagonally across the next field. Do not climb the stile ahead in the far corner but turn sharp left along an enclosed path. After climbing a stile to reach a T-junction, turn right along a track that descends to a farm.

Pass to the right of the farmhouse and where the track bends right, keep ahead through a hedge gap and immediately turn right onto another disused railway track. The track bends right to the parallel track – now a tarmac lane – and you turn left along it, bending right to a road. Turn left and, at a roundabout, turn left through a kissing gate onto a tarmac track, here temporarily picking up the previous route. Retrace your steps over the railway bridge but then keep ahead to a T-junction. Turn right and at the bridge over the River Sow, turn right onto the riverside path. Here you join the outward route and retrace your steps to the start.

## Features of Interest:

**A.** There are a number of fine buildings of various periods and styles in Stafford town centre which are passed on the first part of the walk. On one side of the Market Square is the Shire Hall, an elegant Classical structure built in 1798. Nearby is the Ancient High House, built in 1595 for the wealthy Dorrington family. It is an outstanding example of Elizabethan architecture and claims to be the largest timber-framed town house in the country. It is now used as a museum, exhibition centre and tourist information centre.

Shire Hall, Stafford

Stafford is unusual in possessing two Norman churches. The oldest, St Chad's, dates from around the middle of the 12th century. The Collegiate Church of St Mary, a large and imposing cruciform building, was begun around 1190. The octagonal tower was built in the 15th century.

**B.** Doxey Marshes comprises 360 acres of marsh, wetland and grassland in the Sow valley, a valuable area of greenery sandwiched between Stafford's suburbs and a main railway line. Much of it is a local nature reserve owned by the Staffordshire Wildlife Trust.

**C.** Stafford Castle, once the seat of the Earls of Stafford, occupies a fine vantage point and makes an impressive sight but the ruins that you see are not of the medieval castle – however authentic they look – but of a 19th-century rebuilding. The Normans constructed a motte and bailey castle, probably soon after the Battle of Hastings, and in 1347 a stone keep was built. After the Civil War the castle was abandoned and demolished and then it was partially rebuilt – in the medieval style – in 1813. This was never completed and also fell into ruin. A series of information panels enables visitors to find out about the chequered history of the castle and there is a Visitor Centre.

# 25. Cannock Chase

**Start/Parking:** Cannock Chase Country Park Visitor Centre, Brindley Heath, signposted from A460 at Hednesford — grid ref. 004154

**Distance:** 8½ miles (13.7km)

**Category:** Fairly strenuous

**Refreshments:** Drinks and light snacks at Visitor Centre

**Terrain:** Forest and heath, good tracks and paths throughout

**OS Maps:** Landranger 127, Explorer 6 (to be renumbered 244)

**Public transport:** None

## Discover:

The woodland and heathland of Cannock Chase is one of the most popular walking areas in the Midlands, with miles of attractive and tranquil paths and tracks. This route takes in the three main constituents of the chase landscape — conifer forest, heathland and broadleaf woodland — and includes a stroll through Brocton Coppice, the finest remaining area of oak woodland in the chase, and the beautiful Sherbrook Valley.

## Route Directions:

Begin by passing to the left of the Visitor Centre (A), turn left along a tarmac drive and turn right at a T-junction. At the next T-junction, turn left to a road, walk along it and just before reaching a crossroads, bear right onto a path and cross a road to the right of the crossroads. Take the path ahead through trees, here joining the Heart of England Way, and for most of the first part of the walk you follow the regular Heart of England Way signs. Turn right at a T-junction, take the first turning on the left and continue through the conifers. At the next T-junction turn right, again take the first turning on the left and continue to a road. Keep straight ahead along a track which gently descends to another T-junction. Turn left and after passing beside a barrier, a brief detour to the right brings you to the Katyn Memorial (B). Continue to a road but just before emerging onto it, turn right onto a path that initially keeps parallel to the road but then continues through woodland and across open heathland. At this point there are fine views ahead over the Trent valley.

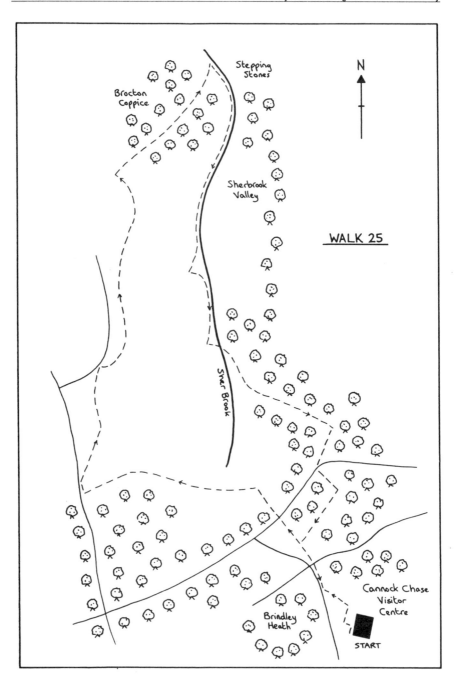

N

Stepping Stones

Brocton Coppice

Sherbrook Valley

WALK 25

Sher Brook

Cannock Chase Visitor Centre

Brindley Heath

START

On reaching a road, turn right through Chase Road corner car park and at a Heart of England Way sign, turn left onto a path which ascends gently to a crossroads. Turn left, continue along a track, passing to the right of a trig point, and at a fork, take the left-hand track which descends to a junction. Keep ahead to reach a car park, turn right to walk through it and at the far end, pass beside a barrier and continue through the trees. At a fork, take the right-hand path which bears first right and then curves left and heads gently downhill through the ancient oak woodland of Brocton Coppice (C) to the Stepping Stones, a popular picnic site in the Sherbrook Valley.

Do not cross the stones but turn right onto a track through the valley, one of the most beautiful parts of the chase, keeping beside the Sher Brook. Follow the track around left and right bends and continue as far as a crossroads. Turn left – there is a sign here 'Short Route to Visitor Centre' – cross stepping stones over the brook and keep ahead along an uphill track through conifers. Pass beside a barrier, keep ahead to a crossroads – by a Cannock Forest notice – and over to the left is the site of an Army Training Camp and disused World War I rifle ranges and butts. Turn right along a broad track to a road, take the path opposite, signposted as a public bridleway and cycle way, and turn sharp right at a junction of tracks, still on the cycle way.

The track keeps in a straight line and on reaching a track and public bridleway sign on the right, you rejoin the outward route. Take the first turning on the left and retrace your steps to the start.

## Features of Interest:

**A.** The medieval royal forest of Cannock covered a vast area, stretching roughly from the Trent valley in the north to Wolverhampton and Walsall in the south, and from Tamworth in the east to Stafford in the west. In 1290 about one-quarter of it – the manors of Rugeley and Cannock - was given by Edward I to the bishops of Lichfield as their private chase and in the 16th century the chase was acquired by the Paget family. It was the Pagets (later the marquises of Anglesey) who played a major role in the exploitation of the mineral resources of the area - iron and coal - and from the 16th century onwards, much of the ancient forest was felled and large areas reverted to bare heath. During the First and Second World Wars, this heathland provided ideal terrain for troop training and several army camps were built, plus a military hospital and a German prisoner of war camp. Brindley Heath, where the walk begins, was the site of a military camp and a reminder of those days is the nearby Commonwealth and German war cemeteries.

From the 1920s onwards, much of the chase was taken over by the Forestry Commission, which established large conifer plantations, chiefly of Scots and Corsican pine. As a result, nowadays Cannock Chase is mainly a mixture of conifer forest and open heathland but some splendid remnants of ancient broadleaf woodland survive, especially in the northern and western parts of the chase which form the country park.

**B.** This was erected by the Anglo-Polish Society as a monument to the Poles who were massacred in Katyn Forest in 1940.

**C.** Brocton Coppice is the finest area of ancient oak woodland remaining in Cannock Chase. As you walk through it, pause to admire the gnarled old oaks – many hundreds of years old – splendidly set off by the masses of silver birches. Much of the coppice and the Sherbrook Valley is a Site of Special Scientific Interest.

Brocton Coppice – the largest remaining area of oak woodland in Cannock Chase

# 26. Chasewater

**Start/Parking:** Chasewater Country Park, signposted from A5 near Brownhills – grid ref. 040071

**Distance:** The full walk is 4 miles (6.4km); the shorter version, which omits the detour around the Wyrley and Essington Canal, is 3¼ miles (5.2km)

**Category:** Easy

**Refreshments:** None

**Terrain:** Mostly across heath and grassland and through woodland encircling a lake; expect some muddy stretches

**OS Maps:** Landrangers 128 and 139, Explorer 6 (to be renumbered 244)

**Public transport:** Buses from Brownhills, Hednesford, Cannock and Walsall

## Discover:

This pleasant walk, mainly comprising a circuit of Chasewater, takes you through a post-industrial landscape, largely reclaimed from colliery waste, and is a good example of how areas of industrial dereliction can be made attractive again. It also includes a short stretch of the Anglesey branch of the Wyrley and Essington Canal. The route is across heath and grassland and through woodland, and from many points there are fine views across the lake.

## Route Directions:

Leave the car park, turn left along a tarmac track and cross a bridge to the dam wall of the reservoir (A). Keep ahead along a path beside the wall for the shorter walk but for the full route, turn right to pass beside a barrier and walk along an embankment above the canal. At the remains of the former Anglesey Wharf, where coal used to be loaded onto canal barges, follow a narrow path to the right across heathland. The path later bears left to keep briefly parallel to a lane and then continues across the heath to reach a road by a canal bridge. Turn left to cross the bridge and at a Cycle Way sign, bear left onto a path which descends to the towpath of the Wyrley and Essington Canal (B). Follow this to the end of the canal and turn left up a tarmac track to the dam wall.

Turn sharp right beside it – here rejoining the shorter walk – and

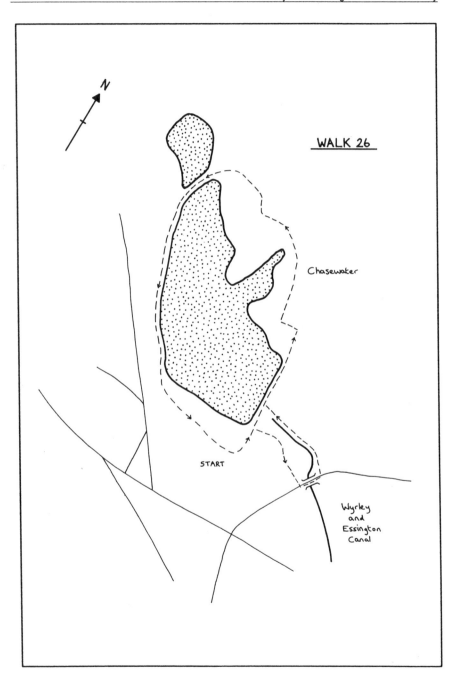

WALK 26

Chasewater

START

Wyrley
and
Essington
Canal

where the wall ends, follow the path which bears left through trees and bushes and across grassland to a tarmac track. Cross it, take the path opposite, turn left at a crossroads and, at a footpath sign, turn left again onto a path into trees. Continue along the right edge of woodland to the lakeshore where you turn right. The path heads uphill, curves left on reaching another path and continues above the lake.

Look out for where a footpath sign directs you to turn left. Descend steps to cross a bridge over a stream and keep ahead across grassland, following a succession of footpath signs, to a junction. Turn right, turn left across grass at the next footpath sign and turn left again at a T-junction. After passing under electricity pylons, turn left to walk beside the track of the Chasewater Light Railway. This provides short trips for visitors at weekends and bank holidays, using one of the former colliery lines. As you cross a causeway over the lake, there is a grand view over the water.

Continue along a broad track by the lakeshore, which curves left to return to the start.

Chasewater

## Features of Interest:

**A.** The area around Chasewater was originally woodland and heathland, part of Cannock Forest, and Chasewater itself was a natural lake called Norton Pool. In 1797 a dam was constructed in order to turn it into a feeder reservoir for the nearby Anglesey Branch of the Wyrley and Essington Canal. During the early 19th century, large scale coal mining started and the canal – and later on the local railways – were used to transport the coal. Mining ceased in the 1950s and, during the 1970s and 80s, much of the scarred landscape was restored and it became a recreational area and waterside pleasure park. Since 1998 it has been designated a Country Park

**B.** Chasewater feeds the Anglesey Branch of the Wyrley and Essington Canal which was built in the late 18th century to transport coal from the mines around Chasewater to fuel the industries of Birmingham and the Black Country. The canal declined and fell into disuse after the coming of the railways.

# 27. Berkswell

**Start/Parking:** Berkswell, car park in village centre – grid ref. 245791

**Distance:** 7 miles (11.3km)

**Category:** Moderate

**Refreshments:** Bear Inn and Post Office Tearoom at Berkswell

**Terrain:** Tracks and field paths across fairly flat terrain but there are – give or take one or two – 50 stiles to negotiate!

**OS Maps:** Landranger 139, Explorer 221

**Public transport:** Buses from Solihull and Balsall Common

## Discover:

This pleasant, tranquil and entirely rural walk is in an area of open countryside that lies between Birmingham and Coventry and only occasional distant glimpses of tower blocks give any indication of the proximity of those two large cities. Berkswell, the starting point, is a most attractive and unspoilt village and its church is one of the finest in the Midlands, with several unusual and distinctive features.

## Route Directions:

Begin by turning right out of the car park alongside the triangular village green (A). At a waymarked post, turn left along an enclosed path, passing under an arch at the side of a bungalow, and continue to a stile. Climb it, keep ahead to climb another and walk along the right edge of two fields, climbing a stile. In the second field, look out for where you turn right over a stile and turn left to continue along the left field edge. Follow the edge to the right, turn left over a stile and keep by the left field edge towards a farm. After climbing a stile, pass to the left of the farm buildings, bear slightly left in front of a gate and continue along a right field edge. Climb a stile in a fence, continue along a track – Ram Hall is to the right – to a lane, cross over and climb the stile opposite.

Walk across a field, cross a footbridge in the corner and continue across the next field. Climb a stile, immediately go through a gate and walk along an enclosed path, eventually turning right and then left over a stile to emerge onto a lane. Turn right, turn left over a stile and walk along a tree-lined path to climb another stile. Keep ahead to climb two more in quick succession, continue along an enclosed path and climb a stile in front of a railway line. Turn left alongside the line, climb a stile onto a lane, turn right to cross a bridge over the railway and on the other side, turn right over another stile and continue along a fence-lined path.

Climb a stile, keep ahead to descend through a belt of trees, walk along an enclosed path and after climbing a stile, cross a footbridge and keep straight ahead across the next field to climb a stile on the far side. Turn left along the left field edge, climb two stiles – crossing an intervening plank footbridge – keep along the left edge of the next field and climb a stile. Bear right diagonally across a field, climb a stile, keep along the left edge of the next two fields, climbing another stile, and in the corner of the second field, make sure you climb the stile in front and not the one to the left.

Walk along the left field edge and turn left over a stile in the corner. The route continues to the left but for a short detour to see Berkswell Windmill, turn right along an enclosed path, go through a gate and keep ahead to a road. Turn left, turn right along Windmill Lane and the windmill is about ¼ mile (0.4km) along the lane (B). Retrace your steps to the enclosed path and continue along it, turning right to cross a plank footbridge and climb a stile. Walk along the left edge of a field, climb a stile onto a road, keep ahead and just before the road bends right, turn left, at a public footpath sign, along a track. Bear slightly right in front of a gate to continue along a narrow, enclosed path which bends right to a stile. Climb it, walk along the left field edge, climb a stile in the corner, cross a plank footbridge and keep along the left edge of the next two fields, climbing a stile. In the corner of the second field, climb a stile, ascend steps, cross a disused railway track and descend steps on the other side to a stile.

Climb it, keep ahead across a narrow field, go through a hedge gap and walk along the left edge of the next field. Climb two stiles – there is another intervening plank footbridge – keep by the left edge of a field, climb a stile in the corner and walk along an enclosed track. Look out for where you turn right over a stile, head across rough grass, climb a stile and keep ahead to climb another one onto a tarmac drive. Turn right to a road, turn left to cross a railway bridge, follow the road to a T-junction, turn right and at the next T-junction, turn left.

Almost immediately turn right over a stile, at a public footpath sign, and walk along the right edge of a field. At a hedge corner, keep ahead across the field, pass through a hedge gap and bear slightly right across the next field to climb a stile on the far side. Walk along the right field

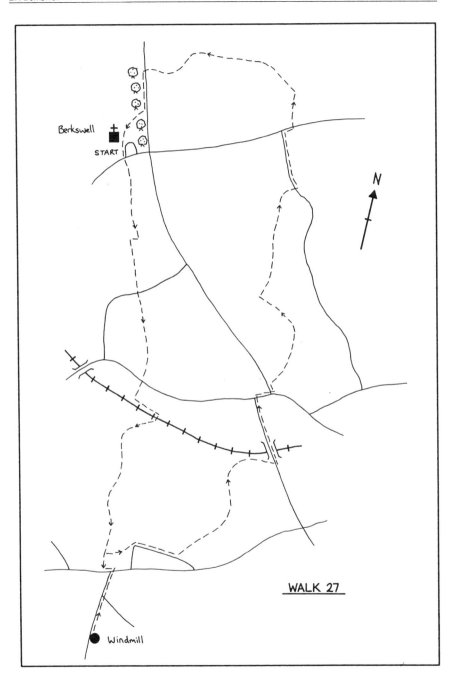

Berkswell

START

WALK 27

N

Windmill

edge, go through a hedge gap and keep along the right edge of the next field. At a footpath sign, turn left across the field, later continuing along the right edge. Go through a hedge gap, walk along the right edge of the next two fields, climbing a stile, and in the corner of the second field, turn right over a stile. Keep along the right edge of the next field, look out for where you turn right over a stile and turn left to continue along a left field edge. At the corner of the hedge on the left, bear slightly right to continue across the field to another hedge corner and keep along the right edge. Follow the edge to the left, turn right over a stile and keep ahead along a drive to a road. Turn left, at a T-junction turn right and at a public footpath sign, turn left along the track to Hill House Farm. At a fork, take the left-hand track, climb a stile and turn left to keep along the left field edge.

After climbing a stile in the corner, turn left along the edge of the next field, follow it as it curves right and in the field corner, keep ahead along a track. Go through a gate to the left of a cattlegrid and continue along the track which curves gradually left, heads gently downhill and later bears right down to a road. Turn left and, just before reaching the first cottages on the left, turn right through a kissing gate and walk along a path through trees to a stile.

Climb it, keep along the left edge of a field – to the right is a fine view of the early 19$^{th}$-century Berkswell Hall – climb another stile in the corner and keep ahead to go through a kissing gate into Berkswell churchyard. Walk along its left edge, go through another kissing gate onto a road and turn left alongside the village green to the start.

**Features of Interest:**

**A.** Berkswell is a most attractive village with old cottages grouped round a triangular green and the pub nearby. The church – a rare example of an almost complete Norman village church – is delightful and has several distinctive features. Perhaps the most striking, and certainly the most picturesque of these is the two-storied, timber-framed 16$^{th}$-century south porch. The upper room was originally the priest's room but has subsequently been used as the village school, a meeting place for the parish council and now a vestry. Apart from the porch and the tower, the latter rebuilt in the 15$^{th}$ century, most of the rest of the church dates from the 12$^{th}$ century. The interior is dominated by the impressive Norman chancel arch and make sure that you visit the well-preserved 12$^{th}$-century crypt, an

Norman church at Berkswell

unusual feature in a small village church and an outstanding example of Norman architecture.

**B.** Berkswell Windmill was built in the early 19<sup>th</sup> century on the site of an earlier post mill.

# 28. Waseley Hills and Lickey Hills

**Start/Parking:** Waseley Hills Country Park, North car park – grid ref. 973783

**Distance:** 7 miles (11.3km)

**Category:** Fairly strenuous

**Refreshments:** Café at Waseley Hills Country Park Visitor Centre, café at Lickey Hills Country Park Visitor Centre, café by Lickey Hills Golf Club car park next to the Old Rose and Crown Hotel

**Terrain:** Hill walking on mainly clear and well-defined paths and tracks

**OS Maps:** Landranger 139, Explorer 219

**Public transport:** None – but you could start from Lickey church which is served by buses from Halesowen and Bromsgrove

## Discover:

The route traverses two attractive and compact ranges of well-wooded hills, separated by the busy A38 (Birmingham-Worcester road), that lie on the south-western edge of Birmingham. They provide the nearest hill walking to the city and, not surprisingly, have long been popular weekend destinations. The views from the highest points – the summits of Bilberry, Beacon and Windmill hills – are both extensive and contrasting, taking in a large slice of rural Worcestershire and ranging across the suburbs of Birmingham and the edge of the Black Country.

## Route Directions:

From the Visitor Centre, make your way across to a footpath post and kissing gate. Go through the gate, turn right along the right edge of a field, in the Clent Hills direction, and look out for where you turn right over a stile, following North Worcestershire Path waymarks. Almost immediately turn left over another stile, continue along the right edge of the next field, go through a gate and keep ahead to a lane. Bear left to a farm and at a T-junction, turn left along a hedge-lined track. In front of a gate, follow the track around a left bend, heading gently downhill, and ford a small brook to reach a gate.

Go straight ahead and, at a fork immediately ahead, take the right-hand path. Go through another gate and keep ahead, passing in front of a house, to go through another. Cross a concrete drive, go

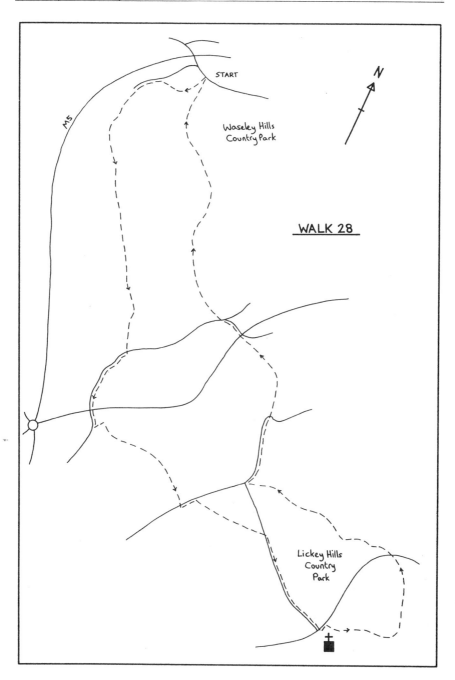

START

M5

Waseley Hills
Country Park

N

WALK 28

Lickey Hills
Country
Park

through a gate and continue along a pleasantly tree-lined and gently ascending track. Where the track turns right down to a farm, keep ahead over a stile and walk across a field, making for the far right corner where you climb a stile into a wood.

Continue through the wood, leave it by another stile and bear slightly left across a field to go through a kissing gate on the far side. Keep by the right edge of the next field and after the hedge bears right, continue straight ahead to a concrete track by a hedge corner. Cross it, keep in the same direction and climb a stile onto a lane. Turn right, follow the winding lane under the A38 and at a right bend, turn first left (No Through Road sign here) and then turn right, at a public bridleway sign, onto a gently ascending tarmac track.

Pass in front of a cottage, go through a gate into woodland and continue uphill. Pass to the right of a small pool, continue along a track by farm buildings to a lane and turn left. At a waymarked stile by a National Trust sign, turn right and then bear left across a field, making for the corner of woodland. Climb a stile, continue across the next field, climb another stile, pass through a belt of trees and cross a tarmac drive to a stile. Climb it, walk across a field, climb another stile onto a lane, turn right and follow the lane to a crossroads. Turn left by Lickey church (A) and turn right along Warren Lane to the Lickey Hills Visitor Centre. On entering the car park, immediately turn left onto a path, between trees, which curves left to join a well-surfaced ridge path over Bilberry Hill (B).

After passing a superb viewpoint looking towards Beacon Hill – reached a little further on the walk – the path descends steeply, via a flight of steps, (the 'Hundred Steps') to a road. From here most of the rest of the route is on the well-waymarked North Worcestershire Path. Cross the road into the gardens of the Old Rose and Crown Hotel and follow North Worcestershire Path signs through the gardens to emerge into the car park at the back of the hotel. Walk through it, passing to the right of the club house and café, and continue steadily uphill, by a fence and hedge on the right.

At the end of a meadow, climb steps through a belt of trees, turn right to a T-junction, turn left and then turn right at the next North Worcestershire Path post. Continue through trees, at the second North Worcestershire Path post turn left steeply uphill to emerge into open country by a trig point and continue across grass to the castellated viewfinder on the summit of Beacon Hill. At 975 feet (298m), this is the highest point on the Lickeys and a magnificent viewpoint.

Continue past the toposcope to the corner of woodland and keep by the left edge of the trees to a lane. Turn right downhill, in the Rubery direction, and just before the lane bends sharply right, bear slightly left onto an attractive, tree-lined, steadily descending path. As you continue along what becomes a tree-lined track, there are fine views to the right across Rubery to the prominent landmark of Frankley Beeches. The Waseley Hills can also be seen ahead. On reaching a road, turn left to cross the A38 and at a T-junction, turn left along Holywell Lane.

Turn right into the South car park of the Waseley Hills Country Park and at the far end, keep ahead beside a barrier along an uphill path. Take the right-hand path at a fork, head up to go through a kissing gate and continue uphill to a fence corner and the edge of trees. Bear right on joining another path and continue over the hill, gently descending to a kissing gate in the field corner. Go through, keep ahead to go through another and continue over the open, grassy slopes of Waseley Hill.

Keep ahead along a superb ridge path, climbing gently to the viewfinder on Windmill Hill, another grand viewpoint (C). From here, bear slightly left to a North Worcestershire Path post in an old hedgeline, descend steps and continue down to the start.

## Features of Interest:

**A.** In the churchyard of this Victorian church is the grave of Herbert Austin, first Baron Longbridge, one of the great pioneers of the British car industry. He founded the Austin Motor Company and built his car works at Longbridge, just down the road from here at the base of the Lickey Hills.

**B.** Since Victorian times the Lickey Hills have been a favourite recreation area for the people of Birmingham and in the 1860s, Elihu Burritt, the American consul in Birmingham at the time, wrote: 'there are no hills more grateful and delightful for airing one's body and soul than the Lickey cluster'. During the Middle Ages, the hills belonged to the manor of Bromsgrove but in the 16th century the area was granted by the Crown to the Earls of Plymouth. The first part of the Lickeys was given to the city in 1888 and over subsequent years, purchases from the Earls of Plymouth and a series of gifts from the Cadbury family extended the area.

The Lickey Hills were probably at their most popular between the wars and in the years just after the Second World War. Most people did not own cars then and on fine weekends and bank holidays,

Beacon Hill, highest point on the Lickeys

thousands of Brummies used to flock here by tram. The present country park comprises 524 acres of mixed woodland, heathland and grassland and has a series of superb viewpoints.

**C.** The Waseley Hills, part of the range that runs along the southern fringes of Birmingham and the Black Country from the Lickeys to Kinver Edge, comprise 150 acres of mainly open hillside with small areas of woodland. They make excellent walking country and the impressive views, especially from Windmill Hill, are both varied and extensive.

# 29. Clent Hills and Hagley Hall

**Start/Parking:** Clent Hills Country Park, Nimmings Visitor Centre – grid ref. 938807

**Distance:** 5 miles (8km)

**Category:** Moderate

**Refreshments:** Refreshment kiosk at Visitor Centre

**Terrain:** A walk through well-wooded and hilly country, with two ascents and descents

**OS Maps:** Landranger 139, Explorer 219

**Public transport:** The walk can be started from Hagley, which is served by buses from Birmingham, Halesowen and Kidderminster

## Discover:

With their sloping woodlands, breezy heights, grand ridge walks and extensive views, the Clent Hills have long been a favourite weekend destination for the people of Birmingham and the Black Country. The first hill that is climbed is just outside the Clent range; this is Wychbury Hill, site of an Iron Age fort. From there the route descends into Hagley, continues by Hagley Hall and then climbs to the Four Stones on the summit of Adam's Hill. After descending to the isolated St Kenelm's church, a short walk leads back to the start.

## Route Directions:

Facing the Visitor Centre, descend the steps to the right of it, go through a kissing gate and walk across a field to go through another one. Continue through a spinney, go through a kissing gate and head gently downhill across the next field to a stile on the edge of Hagley Wood.

Climb it, immediately turn left over another and walk diagonally across a field, looking out for where a path leads off into the wood – this is not easy to spot but is about half-way along the right field edge. Continue gently downhill through the trees and in the corner, turn left onto a track to emerge from the wood. Walk along the right edge of a field, follow the edge to the right, later picking up a track, and just after meeting another track, turn right over a stile. Head diagonally across a field and climb a stile onto the busy A456. Cross carefully, turn left to a roundabout and at a public footpath sign, turn right and descend to a stile.

After climbing it, bear left diagonally across a field towards Wychbury Hill and on the far side – ignoring a worn path on the left – head steeply up the slopes of the hill, making for an obelisk (A). Pass to the right of it to reach the edge of woodland at a stile. Do not climb it but turn left to walk along the left edge of the trees, descending to a stile. Climb it, keep ahead across the slopes, climb a stile onto a track and continue along the enclosed tarmac track opposite to reach the A456 again at Hagley.

Cross over, turn right, take the first road on the left (School Lane) and follow it around a right bend to a T-junction. Turn left – Hagley Hall and church can be seen to the left – and at a T-junction by the entrance to the hall, keep ahead along a fence-lined path, here joining the North Worcestershire Path. After passing beside a metal barrier, fine views of the facade of Hagley Hall open up on the left (B). Pass beside another barrier, bear left to keep along a fence-lined path and after climbing a stile, the route continues along a hedge-lined path to a T-junction. Turn left onto a wide, hedge-lined path to start the gradual ascent of Adam's Hill.

At another T-junction in front of a wooden hut, turn left along a track, turn right over a stile at a hedge corner and continue gently uphill through woodland, following the regular North Worcestershire Path signs all the time. Climb a stile, turn half-left, heading more steeply up to emerge into open country and at the top, turn left along a broad sandy track to the Four Stones at the summit (C). Passing to the left of the stones, keep on the broad track along the ridge, with sloping woodland on both sides, and at a North Worcestershire Path sign, bear right onto a path through the trees.

The path descends, via steps in places, later joins a track and continues down to pass beside a gate onto a lane. Turn left downhill to St Kenelm's church and at the church car park where the lane curves right, keep ahead through a gate into the churchyard. Just before reaching the church (D), turn sharp left to continue across the churchyard and go through a kissing gate. Keep ahead across a field, pass through a hedge at a waymarked post and continue across the next field to a stile in the far left corner. After climbing it, turn left along a hedge-lined track and at a fork by a waymarked tree, take the right-hand path. Head uphill and climb a stile onto a lane opposite the car park.

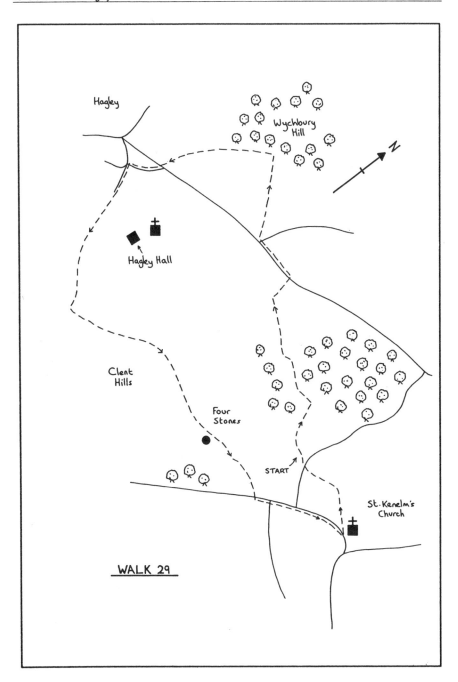

WALK 29

## Features of Interest:

**A.** The obelisk on Wychbury Hill was erected in the 18$^{th}$ century as a landscape feature of Hagley Park. The woodland that crowns the summit of the 734-foot (224m) hill encloses the earthworks of an Iron Age fort built to overlook the Stour valley.

**B.** The elegant Palladian mansion of Hagley Hall was designed by Sanderson Miller, a gentleman architect, for the first Lord Lyttleton. The interior was badly damaged by a fire in 1925 but subsequently restored. There is a fine collection of 18$^{th}$-century furniture and paintings. Close by is the medieval church, heavily restored in the Victorian era. The park contains several follies, including a mock castle and an imitation Classical temple.

Hagley Hall

**C.** Although they look both impressive and authentic, the Four Stones are not a prehistoric monument but were placed here in the 18$^{th}$ century by the first Lord Lyttleton, the builder of Hagley Hall, and his poet friend William Shenstone, who lived nearby at The Leasowes, (See Walk 13) in order to 'improve' the view of the hills. The views from this 997-foot (304m) vantage point hardly need any improvement, extending from the edge of the Black Country across a large slice of the rural Midlands to the outline of the distant Wrekin and the Clee, Abberley and Malvern hills.

**D.** This delightful little sandstone church stands on the site of the alleged martyrdom of St Kenelm, a 9th-century boy prince of Mercia. A spring just beyond the church is supposed to mark the exact spot where the foul deed took place. Although heavily restored in the 19th century, the church still retains much of its original Norman work in the nave and chancel and has a south porch dating from the Tudor period. It was originally just an outlying chapel of Halesowen but in 1841 became the parish church for nearby Romsley.

# 30. Kinver and the Edge

**Start:** Kinver, High Street – grid ref. 845834

**Distance:** 5 miles (8km)

**Category:** Moderate

**Parking:** Kinver

**Refreshments:** Pubs and cafés at Kinver

**Terrain:** Opening stretch along a canal towpath and across fields followed by a short but fairly steep climb onto a wooded ridge

**OS Maps:** Landranger 138, Explorer 219

**Public transport:** Buses from Stourbridge

## Discover:

Starting from Kinver, the first part of the walk is along a short but very attractive stretch of the Staffordshire and Worcestershire Canal. After heading back to the edge of the town, you pass by some of the renowned rock houses before climbing – quite steeply – through woodland onto Kinver Edge. From the glorious ridge path that runs along the edge, the views are outstanding and after enjoying these, you descend, via Kinver's hilltop church, back to the start.

## Route Directions:

The walk starts in High Street in front of Ye Olde White Harte Inn (A). With your back to the inn, turn right, follow the road as it curves left – it becomes Mill Lane – and cross the bridge over the River Stour. In front of the canal bridge, turn left beside a gate onto the towpath of the Staffordshire and Worcestershire Canal by Kinver Lock (B).

Now follows a most attractive stretch of canal walking between Kinver and Hyde Locks and just beyond Hyde Lock – at a blue-waymarked post in front of a cottage – turn left along a tree-lined track. Cross a bridge over the Stour, turn right along a track to a T-junction and turn left, in the Hyde Lane direction. Follow a winding tree- and hedge-lined track to a road and turn left back towards Kinver. At a T-junction turn left along Enville Road, take the first turning on the right (Meddins Lane), head gently uphill and at a Staffordshire Way

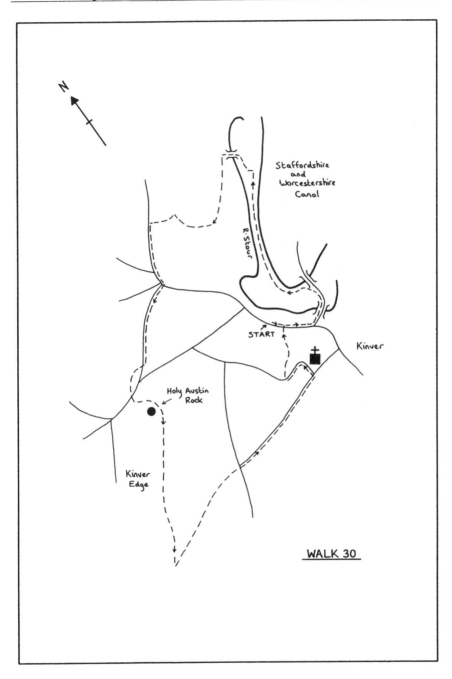

Staffordshire
and
Worcestershire
Canal

R.Stour

START

Kinver

Holy Austin
Rock

Kinver
Edge

WALK 30

sign, bear right beside a barrier and follow a path through woodland to a T-junction.

Turn left, continue gently uphill to a road, cross over and pass beside a barrier at another Staffordshire Way sign. Immediately turn left, head across to a Holy Austin Rock footpath post and continue past it to reach an information board about the Holy Austin Rock Houses (C). Go through a gate, ascend steps, continue beside the rock face and at a corner, turn right to walk beside some of the rock houses. Climb more steps, passing a cave entrance, turn left to descend steps and turn right through a gate. Keep ahead into trees and take the uphill path ahead, bearing left up steps to emerge into an open grassy area. At a footpath post turn right, in the Viewpoint direction, and continue steeply uphill, via more steps, to reach another open area at the top. Here there is a magnificent view and the viewfinder enables you to pick out all the landmarks that can be seen in clear conditions. Turn left at the viewfinder to take the clear ridge path along the top of Kinver Edge (D). The path bears right to re-enter woodland and you keep along it, ignoring all side turns and passing a trig point, as far as a barrier by a Kinver Edge National Trust sign.

Do not go through the barrier but turn sharp left onto a path, by a fence on the right, to a kissing gate. Go through, keep ahead along the right edge of an area of grass, heather and trees, then continue through woodland and go through another kissing gate. Bear right – there is a shelter over to the left – and keep along the right edge of a meadow to pick up a clear path, which emerges onto a road by a parking area. Keep ahead along Church Road and after ½ mile (0.8km), turn left along a narrow lane (Church Hill), passing to the left of the hilltop church, another dramatic viewpoint. The lane bends left and, at a public footpath sign, bear right through a fence gap and head downhill, below a wooded embankment on the left to reach a track. Turn sharp right, passing in front of houses, continue along an enclosed tarmac track and in front of a cottage, turn left and descend steps.

Walk along a tarmac path, passing to the left of a car park, and continue along a track to Kinver High Street. Turn left to return to the start.

## Features of Interest:

**A.** The former iron forging village of Kinver has an attractive High Street with several old buildings. The medieval church – passed near the end of the walk – stands high above the village overlooking the Stour valley. It dates mainly from the 14th and 15th centuries and has a Victorian north aisle.

**B.** For details of the Staffordshire and Worcestershire Canal, see Walk 18.

The Staffordshire & Worcestershire Canal, near Kinver

**C.** The rock houses on Holy Austin Rock are one of several groups on Kinver Edge. In the Victorian period around 12 families lived in them and they became something of a tourist attraction. Some were occupied until as late as the 1950s and even provided teas for visitors. After being closed and falling into disrepair, they were restored by the National Trust in the 1990s. The lower rock houses and caves are sometimes open to the public; contact the National Trust for details.

**D.** It is not surprising that Kinver Edge has long been another of the popular weekend and bank holiday destinations for the people of Birmingham and the Black Country. From this sandstone ridge, covered with woodland and heath, there are the most outstanding and dramatic views: looking eastwards over the Stour valley towards the Clent Hills and the edge of the Black Country, and westwards towards Shropshire. Strategically placed benches enable you to enjoy them in comfort.

# Also from Sigma:

## Discovery Walks in Worcestershire
*Brian Conduit*

Step into Worcestershire's past with this new Discovery Walks guide! Concise but comprehensive information on directions, terrain, degree of difficulty and facilities are given - as well as an informative commentary to enhance your interest and enjoyment. In addition, some longer, more challenging routes are included to satisfy more ambitious or energetic walkers. *£6.95*

## Discovery Walks in Warwickshire
*Dennis Kelsall*

Dennis Kelsall's particular aim in writing this book was "... to encourage walkers to discover more for themselves". Let him guide you towards an exploration of all the county has to offer - wildlife, geology, architecture and history - on his specially designed routes, suitable for all the family. *£6.95*

## BEST TEA SHOP WALKS IN STAFFORDSHIRE
*Clive Price*

Clive Price has chosen a wide selection of walks ranging between 3 and 10 miles and exploiting Staffordshire's vast network of paths and variety of scenery from the Peak District in the North to Kinver Edge in the South. *£6.95*

## WALKING ON & AROUND THE STAFFORDSHIRE WAY
*Geoff Loadwick (Editor)*

16 circular routes that are exhilarating, but not exhausting. The walks, ranging from 4 - 12 miles, illustrate the variety of the Staffordshire countryside: hills, woodland, canal tow paths, and numerous towns and villages of interest. *£5.95*

## LITERARY STROLLS IN AND AROUND THE COTSWOLDS
*Gordon Ottewell*

40 delightful short strolls, with special appeal to lovers of literature and landscape. Discover secret Cotswold corners through the eyes of fine writers, past and present. "With inspirations like J.M. Barrie (Peter Pan), Mary Shelley (Frankenstein), Jane Austen and Dennis Potter, the variety is all-encompassing" COTSWOLD LIFE *£6.95*

## WARWICKSHIRE TOWNS AND VILLAGES
*Geoff Allen*

An invaluable source of information and an absorbing book to dip into, it's also the perfect companion when planning a visit to the county. Immensely readable and well-organised material, revealing the links between the evolution of human history and the vibrant Warwickshire of today. *£8.95*

All of our books are available through booksellers. In case of difficulty, or for a free catalogue, please contact: **SIGMA LEISURE, 1 SOUTH OAK LANE, WILMSLOW, CHESHIRE SK9 6AR.**
Phone: 01625-531035; Fax: 01625-536800. E-mail: info@sigmapress.co.uk
Web site: http//www.sigmapress.co.uk
MASTERCARD and VISA orders welcome.